Susan Alexander is a former tennis champion, successful business woman and a poet.

Susan started playing tennis at 7, won her first tournament at 11 and went on to win many Junior tournaments and long weekend country tournaments during her teenage years.

Between 1967 and 1973 Susan played in Wimbledon twice and won over 30 singles championships and 25 doubles titles in Europe and England. From 1971 - 1973 Sue coached the top Junior girls in Madrid. In 1983 while in Atlanta she gave free tennis clinics to African American children.

In 1975 Sue began working in real estate. Ten years later she started her own business, Sue Alexander Real Estate Pty Ltd, in the back room of her home. The business steadily grew and by the time Sue sold the property management side of the agency in 2006 she was employing nine staff.

A Spanish Love Affair

Susan Joy Alexander

To Genevieve

Enjoy

Susan J Alexander

First published by Susan Joy Alexander in 2017
This edition published in 2017 by Susan Joy Alexander

Copyright © Susan Joy Alexander 2017
https://susanjoyalexander.wordpress.com/
The moral right of the author has been asserted.

The names of some people in this book have been changed and timelines consolidated.

A Spanish Love Affair

POD: 9781925579796
EPUB: 9781925579802

Cover design by Red Tally Studios

Publishing services provided by Critical Mass
www.critmassconsulting.com

For my dear Grandmother Florence from whom I inherited my creative DNA which nearly drove my beloved parents, Thelma and Gilbert mad, my family and friends who have listened to me talk about my book for the past 10 years ad nauseum and my long-suffering husband, Markus Pluss, who has put up with me writing about an affair with another man for the past 10 years.

"Two roads diverged in the wood, and I
took the one less travelled by
And that has made all the difference."
"The Road Not Taken" by Robert Frost

When I gaze at the old black and white photo, I feel very sad. I am 11 and still a child. But I am in love. I feel just like I do as an adult. But I am not ready for love—nor especially, the aftermath. When my tennis coach dumps me for a 14-year-old who wears pancake make-up and goes all the way, I am heartbroken.

PROLOGUE

Last night I dreamt I was in Madrid again.

As I made my way up the Gran Via, I could smell the sun hitting the pavement. The aroma of strong coffee wafted out of sidewalk cafeterias. The familiar dry, musty odour oozed from the vents of the magnificent old buildings lining the street. Sculptures of angels and other winged creatures in carriages appeared ready to launch from atop their roofs.

I was young again!

I tapped my feet on the pavement and raised my arms in the air, clicking my fingers to the flamenco music, belting out in my mind. I felt so alive, so rapturous, as if I was going to burst.

Later on, I wandered through the Museo del Prado. As I entered each salon, my spirit soared when I gazed upon masterpiece after masterpiece—especially Titian's generously proportioned women and Goya's weary dark-robed penitents.

In the late afternoon, I tangoed up and down the length of the living room in our apartment in Chamartin, with my husband, Pedro leading me masterfully, held tightly in his arms while Carlos Gardell's husky voice belted out his heartache.

When evening drew near I wandered down the Calle de los Mesones in the old part of Madrid, where I ate the most delicious tapas and sipped full-bodied Rioja. Afterwards, I danced at The Stones Club with all the boys I've ever known, one after the other, moving to the beat, losing myself in the rhythm, singing the words of soul songs, long forgotten.

It was almost dawn when I walked up my street, General Oraa, clapping my hands for the *sereno* to let me in. He emerged in a cloud of smoke from a nearby cafeteria and bustled self-importantly towards me with his huge bundle of keys to open the front door.

The hallway lights came on. The door on the first-floor apartment opened revealing the old senora, silhouetted in the doorway. She was wearing a quilted dressing gown and teetered on her high-heeled fluffy pink slippers. Her hair, sprouting large rollers, was covered by a chiffon scarf. "*Muy tarde, Senorita Susana. Muy tarde.*" She said tapping her watch.

KING GEORGE V HOSPITAL
23RD FEBRUARY, 1949
6.15AM

I'm squashed in so tightly I can hardly breathe. My body's twisted. My knees are on my nose. My bottom's leading the way. I'm desperate to get out. I push and push. But the space around me feels like it is getting tighter. When I'm about to give up, cold air hits first my body, then my face. I take my first breath and yell for all I'm worth. "Matron," says the nurse. "Look at this beautiful breach. Her name is Susan Joy.

Chapter 1

VAMOS A ESPANA!

EARLS COURT—10th October, 1967—10.30am

I just can't stand another moment in England. If one more drop of rain falls from the dreary, grey sky, I am going to scream. I've been stuck in this bed-sitter for days and am beginning to doubt whether my idea of staying in England over winter instead of going back home to Australia is such a good one.

All the other Australian tennis players have gone home now. Soon I'll have to go out and get a job because my money is running out fast. I hate the thought of being stuck in some dingy cold office, working as someone's secretary. It's certainly not something I am looking forward to. Penny, the girl in the bed-sitter below, tells me that she works as a Bunny and suggests that I too should try out for a job at the Bunny Club! Even though she says that it's great money for very little work, which certainly has a lot of appeal, I really don't fancy walking around in a pair of tights with ears and a powder-puff tail. And anyway, Dad would kill me if he found out. No doubt he would be on the first plane over here.

What makes matters worse is that this morning I received a letter from Australia from my boyfriend Harry. He says he is lonely up at the farm and will have to marry the local schoolteacher, if I don't come home soon.

I too am lonely and feel very tempted. I can imagine getting off the plane on a sunny Sydney day and running into his waiting arms. But I just can't do it! I've changed so much in the short time I've been away. I just know I wouldn't be happy, either on his family property at "Cow Pastures"-via-Charleville, or coaching tennis in Rockhampton. I crumple his letter up and dump it in the bin. He will be much better off with the local schoolteacher.

I also receive a letter from Dawn Fogarty, the captain of this year's Wilson Cup team, (an important interstate Junior competition) wanting me to come home. With Evonne Goolagong and me playing in the singles and Carole Cooper and me in the doubles she thinks we're a cert to win. That settles it. There's no way I'm going home now.

The next day it is still raining and once again the sky is grey and dreary. It is also freezing cold when I finally drag myself out of bed, and still dark, even though it is ten o'clock in the morning. That decides me. I'm not going to stay in London a moment longer. I'm going to Madrid. The Spanish tennis boys I met earlier in the year on the English circuit offered to help me get a job coaching at one of the clubs, and even though I don't like coaching, it will certainly be much better than secretarial work, endlessly cloudy skies and rain.

I pack my bags and head for Victoria Station, without even stopping to check what time the train leaves. I'm in luck: when I arrive at the station, teeming with people, and fight my way through to the ticket office, I find that the train for Madrid is leaving in a couple of hours. I plonk down on a wooden bench to wait, clutching my worldly goods tightly on my lap while I watch all the different types of people coming and going. I find it particularly hard not to stare at the tall, handsome, warrior-like Africans swathed in brilliantly coloured cotton garments striding by. It's certainly very different from Sydney which, due to the White Australia Policy, is predominantly white.

I can only afford to travel second class, so am agreeably surprised when I get into the carriage and find the seats are large and comfortable, albeit old-fashioned. The woodwork is scratched and the leather crackles when I sit down, but it is spotlessly clean. I share the carriage with a few Spanish women who are dressed all in black and say their "Hail Marys" as the train leaves the station. I feel safe riding with their faith.

They smile shyly at me, and I smile back. I can see that they think I am a little strange. They look at me carefully, and then up at my battered suitcase and tennis rackets, then back at me. I am knitting up a storm—I am determined to finish the jumper I am making (quite a difficult pattern) before reaching Madrid and can see they are impressed. We attempt to talk to each other, but even though I have been trying to learn Spanish from a small Penguin textbook (while waiting for the rain to stop during the English tournaments) it is still not very good. They don't speak much English so in the end we manage with a series of signs and smiles. Very kindly they offer to share their lunch of crispy bread rolls, cheese and olives, which they've brought with them in cane baskets covered with red and white checked dishcloths. My stomach has been rumbling with hunger for the last hour and I have to practise a great deal of restraint so as not to make an absolute pig of myself.

It takes two days to get to Spain, which includes the daunting experience of having to catch the Paris Metro from the Gare du Nord station to the Gare de L'Est. I also have to change my English pounds to French francs so I have the money to pay for the ticket. There is no sleeping accommodation in second class but I am out to the world when we are woken in the middle of the night at the Spanish border to have our passports checked and change trains. The Spanish and French gauges are different sizes just like at home between New South Wales and Victoria.

Before our arrival at the Atocha station in Madrid, I revive myself by drinking a very strong double black coffee, loaded with sugar.

From the moment I arrive in Madrid, I feel as if a load has been lifted from my shoulders. It is a stunningly beautiful day. The sun is shining, the sky is cloudless and it is still quite warm, although it is mid-autumn. As I emerge from the station, I have a strong sense that this is where I belong and that I've been here before. My heart aches and tears well up inside me.

I call Antonio Martinez, one of the older Spanish tennis players I met on the tournament circuit, who kindly comes and picks me up at the station. He finds me a place to stay in an old pensione, in Calle de Jacametrezo, a narrow street in the old part of Madrid just off the Gran Via. My room is large and dark with high ceilings and has a small Juliette balcony overlooking a dusty lane.

In the late afternoon, I wander down to the Plaza Mayor. I sit at one of the tables edging the square and sip a *café con leche*. Being in the centre of Madrid enjoying the last rays of the afternoon sun, surrounded by these beautiful old buildings, I am in heaven!

Where's Mummy?

She's gone away! Daddy said she's going to bring a new baby home. I don't want a new baby. Mrs Louks is looking after us. I don't like her. I won't eat anything she cooks. She trips over my toy train, falls down the stairs and breaks her leg. Daddy takes over looking after us, and the cooking. He makes the best mashed potato, with lots of butter and cream. He doesn't make me eat my vegetables like Mummy does. But I still want Mummy back!

Chapter 2

THE ALEXANDER FAMILY

When it comes to parents, my siblings and I won the lottery. Mum told me that when she and Dad decided to get married, the only thing they both really wanted was to have a happy family. Both had experienced difficult childhoods.

Dad's side of the family had arrived in Australia in 1911. My grandfather, John Alexander had been transferred here with Burt, Boulton and Harward, London timber merchants. Florence May, my grandmother, had studied piano at the London Conservatorium of Music. Later she had worked as a secretary at Burt, Boulton and Harward's London office, which is where the couple had met. They came to Australia with their three young sons, Jack 6, my father, Gilbert 4 and James 2.

They were an ill-matched pair. Grandfather John was a dapper man who had his suits made in Saville Row and his shoes sent out from Italy. He managed to avoid the domestic scene as much as possible by taking extended overseas business trips to England and America. Florence, who no doubt found herself in a cultural wilderness in Sydney, was left to keep the home fires burning, for which from all accounts, she was totally unsuited and very unhappy. Her fourth child, Robert was born five months after they arrived in Australia. From then on, she spent most of her time in bed, I believe to avoid any further patter of little feet, until her husband died suddenly one afternoon, of a heart attack at the age of 44, after a game of golf. Dad and his brothers were mainly brought up by an English nanny they all loved dearly. Florence, who was one of ten children, must have been very lonely here in Australia. Although Grandfather John managed to flit back and forth to England on a regular basis, she only managed to go back much later when her youngest son, Robert, attended Harrow College.

On Mum's mother's side, her Great Grandfather John was a second son of a Scottish farmer, who under the law in Scotland didn't stand to inherit. He decided to try his luck in Australia, which was considered a land of opportunity. He immigrated in 1838 under the ten pound pom scheme which offered passage and a land grant. He became a successful landowner in the Walcha area.

Mum's great grandfather on her mother's father's side bought one of the first printing presses in Australia from Sir Henry Parkes. He and his partner moved it from Tamworth to Armidale on the back of a bullock wagon and started the Armidale Express.

Mum's father, Percy George Hipgrave was the editor and owner of the Armidale Express. Prior to his marriage, he was considered a highly eligible bachelor in Armidale and was always a welcome visitor at "Eathorpe" where Norma, Mum's mother, grew up. People thought he was courting one of her elder sisters but he was in fact entranced with the beautiful young schoolgirl who sat on his knee and fed him coconut ice—obviously the way to any man's heart.

Mum's parents were also very unsuited. In fact, their marriage was a disaster. Her father was an intellectual and her mother a beautiful young girl who had hardly ever read a book. With babies arriving non-stop, 14 years' difference in age and nothing in common except for their five children, my grandfather, whose sexual appetite was prodigious, was soon seeking his pleasures elsewhere. My grandmother finally had enough when a smart lady called Miss de Falaise tried to blackmail him and it was reported in the Sydney papers. Grandfather Percy shot through to Adelaide, rather than suffering the ignominy of appearing in court, secretly selling up most of his property with the exception of the heavily mortgaged family home. He disappeared with the proceeds. The scandal which ensued in the small town caused Mum and her siblings a great deal of suffering. They were omitted from guest lists and ignored by previous family friends. People crossed the road to avoid contact with them. Norma, left virtually penniless, moved to Sydney where she worked as a housekeeper—a big come-down from having been a pillar of society in Armidale.

Mum was a woman ahead of her time. After completing two years at teachers' college in Armidale and topping the year, although she'd been offered a place in the newly opened Armidale University, she decided to escape the rancor and vitriol by going down to the city to study for her Bachelor of Arts degree at Sydney Uni. She completed this course at night, working as a teacher during the day. She then planned to go overseas to work. However her plans turned upside down when she met an interesting older man in a boarding house in Petersham with whom she fell instantly and madly in love. Then the war broke out. Mum and Dad "courted" on the tennis court at the boarding house and, I daresay, over numerous cups of tea.

When romance between them blossomed, they dreamed of one day owning a house with a tennis court. Dad also dreamt of having a son who played Davis Cup.

Both these dreams were realised when Dad built a tennis court in the backyard of our family home in Narrabeen on Sydney's Northern Beaches and later on John, my brother, became the number one player in Australia, number eight in the world and the youngest player to represent Australia in the Davis Cup until Bernard Tomic.

Tennis was very close to a religion in our family. It seemed that every spare minute was spent on that court and the major part of our family life revolved around playing or talking about tennis. Initially the family four for doubles was Mum and Dad, my elder sister Annette and me. My brother was not allowed to join in because he did too many double faults and we all got bored waiting for him to get a serve in. That spurred him on no doubt. He spent hours working on his serve, at first on the brick wall just outside the court where we were playing, which was akin to Japanese torture and nearly drove us all berserk.

Although Mum had been an academic, her ambition for me was centred very much on tennis. She always dreamt that John and I would play in the mixed doubles at Wimbledon. Although I competed successfully through the junior ranks, over the years I received mixed messages from both my parents about my future career in tennis, which I found rather confusing. It seemed that they thought that any career I might embark upon would just be something to do for a few years until I got married and had a family.

Dad's dream for me was more of the practical kind.

He was 42 when I was born and knew he wasn't always going to be around to support me. He wanted me to have financial security. Even from an early age Dad was intent on a career in business for me. I received a toy telephone for my third birthday and a cash register for my fourth. When I was seven, he taught me how to write the receipts for the rents for the block of units he owned. Dad hated paperwork and was keen to offload it. He gave me a typewriter for Christmas when I was eleven. When I left school to concentrate on tennis, he insisted that I did a secretarial course. I hated being confined indoors and stuck in a chair—without any wheels in those days—taking down dictation then typing it out all day. I wanted to be outside and on the move. But Dad pressed on. He was determined to get a square peg into a round hole.

I wanted to perform. When I was in 5th class, I had desperately wanted to be a dancer, then when I got too tall to be a ballerina, an actress. Both Mum and Dad were very concerned about my creative side. They were afraid I'd taken after Dad's mother, Florence, who was very musical and arty. She played the piano, sang and wrote fantastic stories. However, she failed to pass muster with either of my parents because she was "on the bohemian side", was constantly on the move, had unreal expectations of life and people, was an unskilled money manager, a hypochondriac without maternal instincts or housewifely skills and smoked 'roll-your-owns'. I adored her.

A BEE STORY

I was climbing
down the stairs
When I was only three
Would you believe I missed my step
And sat down on a bee

I squashed that bee flat
And he died
Then I sat on the step with my head in my hands
And I cried and I cried and I cried

I can still feel that feeling
Of that bee sting on my bum
It was times like this
I was glad to have my mum

So now I'm very careful
Before I sit down
To make sure there's nothing where I'm about to sit
That is small and brown
And goes Buzzzzzzz!

Chapter 3

ME VOY!

I had no idea who I was, where I was going or what I wanted out of life. I only knew what I didn't want! And going overseas to play tennis certainly sounded a lot more interesting a proposition to me, and definitely more fun than banging away at a typewriter in some dreary office.

In 1967, just after my eighteenth birthday, I left Australia on a private tour to play tennis on the European and English circuits. There was no alternative to touring privately because no Australian women's team had been sent overseas since 1955, when Jenny Hoad nee Staley had fallen pregnant on tour. Not that I would have been selected in a team anyway, even if there had been one. I already had a poor record from when I was part of a junior team sent to Melbourne, captained by Gail Sherriff, for the Australian Junior Championships. To kick off, my partner, Carole Cooper, and I were snipped for smoking in the train on the way down. It was our first taste of freedom and we were out to make the most of it much to our team captain's displeasure.

At the time private tours were a haphazard affair. There were no computer rankings so letters had to be written giving details of recent tournament results and requesting an invitation to play. As we players were constantly on the move, replies were often not received. Deals varied. In Europe, the luxury hotels often hosted the tournaments and provided sumptuous accommodation and fabulous meals but nothing to drink except tap water. Other tournaments paid a small amount which had to cover travel, accommodation and living expenses. In England, as I was only 18, I was generally billeted with families, ate my meals mostly at the clubs and was given the exact train fare to the next tournament. Meantime, the men players received much better deals, as well as "appearance money"—most of it secretly negotiated "under the table".

I was very surprised that my parents let me go overseas by myself at such a tender age.

During my teenage years I'd always been kept on a very tight rein. Whenever I went out, Mum and Dad wanted to know with whom I was going and where I was headed. This usually involved a Gestapo-style interrogation. Very strict curfews were in place. I can only surmise that they were totally oblivious of the world I was being catapulted into. There was no SBS, little foreign news and practically no interaction with other nationalities on Sydney's Northern Beaches at that time.

In hindsight, the main reason they may have gone along with the tour was to delay my marriage to my boyfriend Harry. When Harry had asked Dad for my hand, although he was a lovely man and excellent husband material, Dad persuaded him to let me go overseas for a year to play tennis before "settling down". He felt that I was too young and didn't have enough life experience to get married.

Dad lived to really regret that decision!

I'm a Daddy's Girl!

I don't like making beds. When I'm big I'll be like Daddy. Mummy laughs. She says when I grow up I'll have to. No I won't. I'll show her. When Daddy goes out to his truck, I sneak out the door with my red dinky. I follow Daddy up the driveway then start off down the hill. Powder Works Road is very steep. I have to keep my feet on the ground. I can't keep up with Daddy. I get to the bottom of the hill, turn right into Garden Street and am just about to turn onto Pittwater Road when I hear Mummy yelling "Stop!"

Chapter 4

REAL MADRID CLUB DE TENIS

Plaza de Castilla

MADRID

Antonio Martinez is waiting for me by a small gazebo at the side of the main gates of the Real Madrid Tennis Club, where he's organised for me to practise while I'm in Madrid. After he signs me in, we stroll down a long, pebbled drive, elegantly landscaped on both sides, to the club—a substantial two-storey building with ten courts in front of it. As we step inside, there is a pause in the buzz of conversation. People turn around. I blush.

The whole downstairs area is one huge room flooded with sunlight from large casement windows. The one exception is the bar, which is dimly lit and filled with solidly constructed dark wooden tables and chairs. The upper-level dining area, which encircles the outer walls and overlooks the floor below, has the same dark wooden furniture but the tables have starched white cloths and serviettes on them, and are set ready for lunch.

"Most of the club members are wealthy Madrilenos who have known each other for years," Antonio explains. "They are in the fortunate position that they can afford to live off either their investments or earnings from their 'fincas' (country estates), and come here every day to pass the time drinking coffee, having lunch and a game of tennis. Later in the afternoon they play dominoes."

Dominoes! I can't believe it! I smile smugly to myself and don't feel quite so intimidated. I gave that game up when I was six.

Antonio introduces me to a tall American girl, Marlena, who he's organised for me to have a hit with. She tells me that she is from Florida and is living in Madrid with her sister, Angelica, who is studying to be an opera singer. "I've been working as a model but I'm having a weight problem and that's why I want to get back into tennis," she confides.

She turns out to be a very average type of club player so I teach her how to do all the training exercises I learned from Sid Drake, my old tennis coach. At least it allows me to get some kind of workout. When we chat afterwards, she tells me that there are rooms to let underneath the flat where she and her sister live, in Calle General Oraa, a street just off the Serrano in Salamanca. "A much better address than where you're living at the moment," she says, "and it's also much closer to the club."

When we leave, she takes me around to her block and introduces me to an old widow, Dona Ana, who wants to rent out the rooms. I am shown a large, gloomy bed-sitting room that doesn't have any windows. A short way down the hall is a bathroom, which is a lot better than the one at my current address. In my pensione in Calle de Jacamatrezo, I have to share the bathroom with all the other people on the floor, and put up with the tiles always being wet and slimy and the sink full of whiskers.

I am also fed up with having to cough or hoick every time I give taxi drivers my address in an attempt to pronounce the

Spanish "jota". If I use either the soft English "h" sound or the hard "j" they simply refuse to understand me.

Although I will miss the narrow, winding streets, lovely old buildings and especially the Plaza Mayor and the Puerta del Sol, I am a bit lonely all by myself. So I decide to take the rooms.

Narrabeen Infants School
Ocean Street

Mum and I are outside the school gate. It's my first day at school. I don't want to go in, but mum says I have to. It's the law. And anyway, she says that I am bored and lonely at home. I am not! She tells me I'll love school. I will not! I hate wearing this red and white checked dress, white socks and most of all the black shoes. I like bare feet. And I don't like being stuck inside all day either.

Chapter 5

LAS DOS SENORAS

General Oraa 19, MADRID

Every afternoon when I step through the front door of Dona Ana's apartment my eyes take a while to adjust to the dimly lit rooms. I am always greeted by a chorus of *"Buenas tardes, Senorita Susana"* emanating from the dining room. Most weekday afternoons, Senora Dona Ana plays cards with her friend, Senora del Puerto from down the road. The remains of their *merienda* occupy the middle of the card table. It is gossip time. Senora del Puerto loves to shock Dona Ana with her stories. Although I can't understand every word, I can usually get the general gist of what they are talking about by the look on their faces especially when Senora del Puerto is telling Dona Ana a choice piece of neighbourhood gossip. *"No me diga Usted. Que no lo creo. Como puede ser verdad?"* mutters Dona Ana, leaning forward. (Don't tell me. I don't believe it. How could it be true?) Sometimes Senora del Puerto reads the Tarot cards.

Although these two widows have played cards together every afternoon for more than twenty years, they still address each other as "Senora" and speak formally in *"Usted"*. I find this surprising because at the Real Madrid Club everyone uses first names and "tu". It also amazes me how these two have managed to last the distance, because they are so different from each other.

My senora, Dona Ana, is very small and lady-like, a classic Spanish senora. She goes to Mass every morning and, as she is a widow, dutifully dresses all in black, as custom dictates. She has no waistline to speak off, tiny wrists and hands, very slim legs and teeters slightly on her heels. She speaks softly and titters behind her hand when she laughs.

Senora Ines del Puerto, on the other hand, is a robustly built Asturian woman. She thumps around the apartment, speaking loudly and laughing raucously. She is on the bawdy side and often hints at the many young lovers who are pursuing her now that she is a widow. Although most of her clothes are also black, she loves to shock Dona Ana and flout convention by wearing a dashing, brightly coloured scarf around her neck. Her favourite is purple.

What on earth would the two senoras make of my mother, Thelma, who I calculate must be around the same age—running around in her short tennis skirts, whacking the tennis ball with all her might down the sidelines and stopping for a swim in the surf on the way back from shopping? And what would they think of our home in Narrabeen with the sun pouring in, sea breezes gusting through, always the odd sweaty tennis player wandering in and out and a big pile of smelly Dunlop Volley sandshoes at the front door?

Dona Ana and Ines would certainly be surprised at our two-storey home with its large picture windows overlooking the ocean and lake, and big yard complete with chooks, a vegetable garden and a tennis court where, before school, John and I play death matches, with Dad on the umpire stand trying to keep the peace. In Madrid everyone lives in apartments.

Both the senoras are very religious, as it appears is everyone in Spain, albeit that Dona Ana is more regular in her attendance at Mass. Although Mum and Dad duly sent us to Sunday school, I found out later that they were both atheists. They kept this quiet when we were growing up in the 1950s, the era of the American Evangelist Billy Graham, a time when the majority of Australians were Christians (89.4% in 1954) and regular church goers. Thinking back I'm sure Mum and Dad only sent us there so they could have an uninterrupted roll in the hay on a Sunday morning then peace and quiet while they gardened.

On Sunday afternoons, although I'd rather have been on the beach with my surfy boyfriend, Jeff, Mum and Dad insisted I stay home and play social tennis with family friends. Everyone was on first-name terms, with the kids using the honorific Uncle and Aunt before the adults' names. Endless cups of tea were drunk, pikelets, jam and cream eaten, the doings of various family members caught up on and the latest news dissected, all under the shade of the old fig tree. Much to the men's disgust, Mum, a teetotaller, wouldn't let anyone have a beer until after six and then only one, before giving everyone their marching orders!

I think I'm adopted.

I'm not like my sister. She likes playing dolls. I don't. Dolls are boring. She also likes helping Mum. I don't. And she loves school. I don't. I'm not like my brother either. He's happy playing with his dinky toys all day—making engine noises—driving them in and out of his petrol garage. I hate staying still. I like to be on the move – to run barefoot through the bush, and climb trees right to the top. When I do stay still, I feel like I am going to burst.

Chapter 6

LAS HERMANAS FRANGOPOULOUS

It seems that Marlena, the American girl I met at the Real Madrid Tennis Club, and her sister, Angelica, are short of cash. All week Marlena has tried to sell me some of her old clothes. Then she asks me if I would like to come and live with them in their flat, one level above.

I decide to take up her offer because their flat is much nicer than the one where I am living. And although I will have to share the bathroom with the two sisters, the rent is cheaper. Their flat is also not crammed full of ancient furniture, nor dimly lit with an ever-present musty smell. I find life boring at Dona Ana's. She can't speak a word of English, and her little maid, Carmen, who never says anything to me, always scurries away down the hallway muttering under her breath whenever she sees me. Dona Ana is a little put out when I tell her that I am leaving.

After only a week living with the two sisters I realise that I've made a dreadful mistake. Sharing a flat with them is like living on the side of a volcano, particularly with Angelica. Each morning I am woken at the crack of dawn by her singing scales, up and down, up and down which goes on for what seems like forever. Unfortunately, this particular morning, she is having a bad day and is not hitting the high notes cleanly. It becomes increasingly unbearable, akin to when someone scrapes their fingernails down a blackboard. Every now and again she stops, sighs dramatically, swears a bit, and then bangs down on the piano keys before getting back on the job. Around eleven, I hear her going into the kitchen to pour herself a drink. From past experience I know it will be a Scotch. I am also aware that this will not improve matters. She starts singing her way through her repertoire. Opera is definitely not my thing. In fact, I believe I have an inherited antipathy, in particular to coloratura, from my father. He always had to leave the room if it was on the radio! With Angelica's high notes becoming more excruciating by the minute, I too feel I have to get out of there!

Unfortunately, I am not fast enough!

Angelica catches me just as I am about to go through the front door and starts shouting at me. She pulls me towards the kitchen and bops the lid of the kitchen tidy-up and points. "For Christ's sake, can't you flatten your bloody cereal box when you put it into the bin, and wash your cup and plate up and put them away when you goddamn use them? Your bloody lack of housekeeping skills," she screeches, "is driving me berserk."

What can I say? She is in such a filthy mood that I am concerned for my safety. I skedaddle.

When I come back from the shops around twelve, I overhear Angelica and Marlena, who is just about to go out for lunch with a friend, having an almighty row. It seems that Marlena wants to give her date, Eduardo, who is very good looking and in fact the epitome of a dashing Spaniard but unfortunately always low on funds, a glass of Scotch. Angelica is kicking up a hell of a stink about it. The two sisters keep all kinds of wines, liqueurs and spirits under the kitchen sink and have a very precise system in place as to what each visitor gets to drink. This is relative to how generous their guest is with them.

In the end, much to Angelica's consternation, Marlena gives him a small Scotch when, according to Angelica, he is only supposed to be offered the cheap red wine which has been sitting open in the cupboard all week. Angelica is fuming and huffs out of the kitchen, slamming the door behind her.

Later that day, when Marlena comes home she puts on her LP record of Brazil '66, and goes into the bathroom. All I can hear for the next half hour is the gushing of the cistern as the chain is pulled continuously. "Marlena puts her finger down her throat to make herself puke. That's how she keeps her weight down so she can model and still eat whatever she wants," Angelica volunteers.

"Meow, meow!"

A black and white cat came to visit us this morning. Mum says she is half Persian. She is black with white paws and has a fluffy tail. I call her Snow Boots. She lives up the road but Mum told me she saw the kids picking her up by the tail. Mum gives her a bowl of milk. Snow Boots settles down for a snooze in the sun on the old cane lounge. I hope she decides to stay with us. I love stroking her especially when she purrs. The next day she has four beautiful kittens in my cardigan drawer. Dad has given me a nickname – Sucat!

Chapter 7

EL METRO

I'm having so much fun living in Madrid that tennis is taking a back seat at the moment. This is the first time I've ever been free from the constant regime of practising and playing in tournaments and I'm loving it. But my money is running out fast. I don't want to have to swallow my pride and ask Mum and Dad for cash so a couple of days later when I am going to the Prado, I decide to economise by taking the Metro instead of grabbing a taxi.

Train trips always bring back bad memories of Mum hustling me down the platform so I wouldn't miss the train, when I had to return to boarding school.

It is my first time on the Metro in Madrid. The stairs leading down to the platforms are dimly lit and the ceiling is much lower than the Tube in London. I feel like I am entering a cave. Fortunately, I only have to go two stops from Serrano to Plaza de Colon, without any changes of trains. I take a deep breath, steady myself and think of what Dad used to always say to me whenever I faced difficult situations. "You can do it, Sucat!"

The platform is very crowded and everyone steps forward as the train appears out of the tunnel. No sooner has it stopped than the front runners pry the carriage doors open and pile in, causing the poor people trying to get off to have to fight their way through the incoming hordes. I grab the leather strap as the train jolts its way out of the station and elbow a Spaniard who is trying to take advantage of the fact that we are jammed in so tight that my breasts are at his nose level. I then stare down another bloke who in the jostle is trying to rub up against me.

It is then that I notice there is a terrible smell in the carriage. I take several deep breaths before I can make up my mind what it is. I decide, in the end, that it is a combination of yesterday's garlic, hairy underarms, no deodorant and weekly baths, with the odd fart thrown in for good measure.

Only a week later I am on the train again and can't smell anything. Now that is a worry!

May 24TH, 1956
Empire Day at Narrabeen Infants School

The sun's boiling. It's a real scorcher. The edges of the tar playground are soft. I'm wearing a red crepe tunic and hat which Mum has made for me. When the music starts, we all march towards a flag marked out on the playground, then stand in our places according to our colours. We sing "God Save the Queen". The headmistress tells us to bow our heads. "Let us pray for the other nations in the Empire." I wonder whether they'll hear us. Then she prays for a plane to go overhead. "Stand absolutely still children. Imagine what the pilot will think?" After several minutes she gives up. Thank goodness. We can go and stand in the shade at last.

Chapter 8

EL CLUB PICCADILLY

Even with fairly fierce economising, the little money I have is nearly gone. I really have to seriously start looking for a job. So when Angelica tells me that she knows an American guy who is one of the partners at the Piccadilly, my favourite nightclub, and that she will organise a job interview as a dancer for me, I am beside myself with excitement.

The interview goes very well. Somehow I manage to land my dream job. My new boss doesn't even check if I can dance. I can't believe it! Somebody is actually going to pay me to dance. And what's more, I will be dancing to fabulous music because all the most fantastic bands play at the Piccadilly.

I've tried various other jobs—teaching English—but was put off when my student, Manuel, a middle-aged portly Madrileno who never did his homework, thought putting his hand on my knee and sliding it upwards was included in the fee for his lesson. I also find coaching tennis very boring. Mum told me she had to sit down when I told her I was being paid for taking up hems!

I decide not to tell Mum and Dad about this new job though. Even if it might be somewhat of a consolation to them that all the money they'd spent on my ballet and dance lessons when I was young has not been a complete waste. Mum would most definitely not approve, and if Dad finds out, he will be on the first plane over to Madrid.

On my first night I can hardly keep my nerves down to a dull roar. It feels just like I am about to go onto the court to play in an important match. My knees feel weak and those ever-faithful butterflies in my stomach are running wild. I am wearing a very short green brocade mini, which I bought on the Kings Road, which has matching shorts underneath. A dark green silk ribbon threads its way through a strip of white brocade at the bottom of each leg, and ties up mid-thigh.

Before we go on, I meet the other two girls working that night, who I've seen dancing when I've been here before. We dance on three small round pedestals in front of the African-American band the Box Tops. Their fabulous soul music starts with my favourite song by the Four Tops, "Reach out I'll be there". As soon as the music starts and I begin to dance, my nerves disappear. As well as being a fantastic band, they are also fabulous dancers and at the break when I talk to the lead guitarist, he promises to show me how to dance like they do.

Although it is well after four in the morning when we finally finish for the night, we are all still wide awake. We catch a cab down to the old part of town where there are lots of cafeterias still open, serving breakfast for the factory workers and late suppers for the night people—clubbers, artists, actors, writers, dancers, musicians and me! Churros and chocolate are the speciality and the chocolate is so thick it's like a melted Cadbury's block. The only way to eat it is to dunk the churros into it. Probably I'll have enough pimples to last a year after this little lot!

The boys from the band are the centre of attention because there are not many dark-coloured people in Madrid at this time. Franco keeps a lid on immigration in general, and of the coloured/non-Catholic types in particular. So these guys stand out. They are also exceptionally good looking with their shiny skin and lean, muscular bodies displayed to perfection in bright-coloured tight-fitting clothes and their 180 degrees smiles, showing off their magnificent expanses of dazzlingly white teeth. At the end of the night, the lead guitarist who is all of the above wants me to go back to his hotel with him. It is certainly tempting. But no way! I can just imagine Mum and Dad's faces if they found out I was dating a black man.

After dancing at the Piccadilly for three months, I find all the hanging around between sets boring. The management won't allow us to mix with the customers, so I bring my little Spanish grammar book along and try to conquer the subjunctive as I wait in a dark corner. I've become a night person and have hardly seen the light of day since I started. Except sometimes at the wrong end! Usually, by the time I get home from work the sun is already coming up. I sleep most of the day and when I get up around six, the sun has already gone down.

One thing that I don't like at all is that Jean, one of the French managers, is always making sordid remarks, grabbing me from behind, trying to touch me up and generally making a nuisance of himself. He's been eyeing me off for some time. He is a sleaze bag. One evening he asks me to come home with him and his wife for "una copita" (a little drink). I know very well, from previous experience, that there will not be any little cups nor for that matter anything available to drink. When I knock him back, he tells me that his wife will be very disappointed because she really "likes" me. I hold my breath so that I don't crack up as I imagine the scenario. These two deviates licking their lips at the thought of a riotous "ménage a trois", then finding out they had a decidedly inexperienced virgin on their hands. He goes off in such a huff, I can tell that he doesn't like being refused at all.

"You won't last here long after knocking Jean back," one of the other dancers tells me.

And she is right. When I go into work the next day, I am called into the office and given the bullet.

Ouch!

I'm climbing a tree. "You betta get down 'cos I wanna cut it down," Peter Bolton yells as he swings an old tomahawk at the branch I'm on. He hits my foot. I yell loudly. Blood's pouring all over the place. Mrs Bolton comes out. Mum says she has nerves. She goes as white as a sheet. She hoses my foot off, puts a bandage around it then sends John and I home. When mum sees the bandage oozing with blood she piles us into the car. I get six stiches. "You're lucky you still have your foot young lady," Dr Rosati says. "That's the third lot of stitches you've had in it this year."

Chapter 9

TRES ES DIFICIL – CUARTO NO FUNCIONA NADA

Christina, an English girl who I've become friends with, moves in with the American sisters too. They are initially delighted at the thought of the extra money, but before too long things start to go downhill. Although they desperately need our rent money, they tell us we are driving them mad with our noisy late night comings and goings, not to mention our lack of housekeeping skills.

Christina and I find them just as difficult to live with. We both feel we are constantly walking on eggshells. As well as driving us mad with her scales, Angelica is a neat freak and continually picks on us for being untidy. Christina and I both agree that she is much, much worse than either of our mothers! Marlena, on the other hand, is going through a rough patch. She has put on too much weight for modelling and is trying to remedy this by her usual method. She just can't get enough of Brazil '66 and is up in the bathroom throwing up after every meal. Consequently, the bathroom always stinks of vomit and the strong disinfectant which she uses to try to counteract the smell.

I am pretty sure Angelica is trying to get rid of us when she tells me there is a job going as a "live-in" housekeeper for a friend of hers, Bob Barnete, an American artist. I swore blind as a child that when I grew up I wouldn't do housework. I wanted to be like my father and go out to work. But our current impecunious circumstances call for drastic action. Christina thinks that this job could be the answer for us, at least temporarily. She insists that it will be easy, and we'll knock it over in no time. Free rent, she says, is not to be sneezed at. She tells me she's had lots of experience, which I find hard to believe (based on the current evidence), and will show me what to do.

Anyway, we don't have any alternative, because neither of us can stand another moment with the sisters and we are just about broke.

We catch a bus to Bob Barnete's home, which is a fair way out of town, in the middle of nowhere, halfway along the road to the Sierra del Guadarrama. His house is on a large block, surrounded by a high white stucco wall covered in half-dead bougainvillea, in a group of about twenty other homes. These are the only houses I've seen so far in Madrid that are anything like the houses in Sydney. We walk up the path past a pool filled with dead leaves and discoloured water. The front door, which is solid oak, has a large metal door-knocker shaped like a bull, and is answered almost immediately. We are greeted by a stocky, dark-skinned man with very thick black hair, *brylcreamed* into place, a pencil-thin moustache and a decidedly wild look in his eye. He speaks to us in a strong American accent, introducing himself as Bob.

As we step inside it is cool and dark, the walls are white and lined with vibrantly coloured paintings of bullfighters bravely raising their capes towards the oncoming charge of raging bulls, and brilliantly dressed flamenco dancers twirling their bodies and clicking their fingers. He asks if we would like to smoke and offers us Marlboro or hashish. I take a Marlboro.

Bob explains that he is looking for a live-in housekeeper and part of the job is to sleep in his bed with him. He doesn't think it is a problem that there are two of us. "You can take it in turns or sleep one on each side," he tells us. "You'll see I have a huge bed," he continues, edging us towards the bedroom, as though it was the most normal thing in the world. Maybe he is considering giving us a test run.

"We'll think it over and give you a call," I reply as we sidestep around him then hustle out the front door and down the path.

Once outside his front gate, we hightail it down the street as fast as we can until we are puffed out and our sides ache so much that they feel like they are going to burst.

Teacher's Pet

I'm in fourth class. Our teacher is Miss Collins. She is short, stocky and cranky. She strides across the playground, bent over with her head forward. She looks like a dragon. Any moment I expect her to roar and smoke to come out of her mouth. She raps Christine Cook across the knuckles most mornings because her desk is crooked. At lunchtime she makes me stay in the classroom while she undoes my plaits, combs my hair and then re-plaits it. She says my hair is like silk. I hold very still. I am scared if I move in the slightest she will hit me with her ruler. The other girls in the class say I'm teacher's pet.

Chapter 10

UNA PROTESTA DE LOS ESTUDIANTES

The clubhouse at the Real Madrid is all abuzz when I arrive. People are huddled in groups, whispering together. No one is playing tennis nor even dominoes. I corner Marina to find out what the kafuffle is about. In a student march the previous day, four students have been killed and many injured or arrested, she confides. I breathe a huge sigh of relief that I hadn't gone with Antonio, one of my friends at the Real Madrid Club. He is head of the student body at the university and speaks Spanish very, very fast without opening his mouth so I often catch very little of what he says. I definitely didn't get the finer points of his conversation on this particular occasion. It was something about how the students were going to march as a protest and then go on strike. But for what, I had no idea.

He invited me to come along but luckily for me I had something else on that day, because from all reports, the Guardia de Civil came down on the heavy side, riding roughshod on horseback right over the students and bashing them with their batons.

The students were young, naïve and foolhardy, seemingly unaware that in 1967 they were living under such as an oppressive regime. Franco, often referred to as *El Caudillo* (the leader/boss), had ruled Spain with an iron fist since 1939. His rule was law. He dealt ruthlessly with anyone who opposed him. All sorts of austere measures had been implemented and he systematically suppressed dissident views through censorship and coercion, imprisoned ideologically opposed enemies, and used the death penalty and heavy prison sentences as a deterrent.

In the short time I've been in Spain I'd already noticed that *nobody* ever discussed politics openly. Nor did they make fun or have a laugh at Franco's expense. The ominous presence of this right-wing dictator hovered in back rooms, taxis, restaurants and private homes in the form of a multitudinous web of spies purported to be lurking, listening and reporting back about anyone who spoke in opposition to him.

16th September 1956
TCN CHANNEL 9

Our lounge is full. Everyone from Powder Works Road is here. Except Dad. He's gone to watch the Olympics in Melbourne. That's why he's bought us a television set. Mum turns the switch on. There's a man's face on the screen, just like at the pictures only smaller. His name is Bruce Gyngell. "Good evening. Welcome to television," he says. No one can believe it. It's magic! Right here in our living room. Dad has also left a television running in his electrical appliance shop at Narrabeen. Every night over 100 people bring their chairs down and watch our athletes perform magnificently. We come third—winning 35 medals.

Chapter 11

OTRO TRABAJO

Marlena has come up with another possible job for me as a shop assistant at a gift shop selling Spanish artefacts out at Torrejon. She tells me that the owner of the business is looking for someone who can speak English because a lot of his customers are Americans from the air base nearby. I am desperate for money so I ring the number that Marlena has given me and organise an interview.

When I arrive, Peppi, the owner of the shop, doesn't bother with any questions as to whether or not I have any experience working in a shop; nor does he look me in the eye when he talks to me. Instead he just gives my body a quick once over, then appears to talk to my right breast. He tells me that I have the job. I know he is pure *slime*, but I really do need the job as Angelica and Marlena are on my back about the rent, so I decide to hang in and at least give it a go.

Anyway I've always wanted to work in a shop. One of my favourite games as a child was setting up "shop" on the footpath in front of the house. When Dad gave me a toy cash register, I was in heaven.

I particularly enjoy serving the customers, most of whom are from the air base and speak English albeit with strong American accents. Yesterday a couple of nice American blokes, Charles and Harry, who were looking for presents for their family back home, came in and bought heaps of stuff. I've arranged to meet up with them again.

Unfortunately I am right about Peppi. He turns out to be an absolute pain. All week he tries to touch me up. I am absolutely at the end of my tether. That man just can't keep his hands to himself. He is constantly grabbing at me, especially whenever I go upstairs to the storeroom. One morning towards the end of the week, it is the last straw! When a very nice American lady, after considerable deliberation, decides to buy a Spanish flamenco doll, Peppi sends me upstairs to get the replica.

As usual, no sooner do I get up there, he mounts the stairs in hot pursuit and tries to grab me. But he is out of luck because it is a bad time of the month and I have a very short wick. I am in no mood for Peppi's overtures. So instead of telling him to piss off, like I usually do, I start to run round and round the storeroom. Goodness knows what the poor customer must be thinking, with the terrific racket going on upstairs, as we pound around in circles, sending stock crashing to the floor. In the end I run down the stairs, pausing barely long enough to catch the startled expression on the American woman's face, then out the door and down the street.

I keep running for several bus stops.

Grandma Alexander

I love visiting Grandma. She doesn't live in a house. She doesn't like houses she tells me—nor housework for that matter. Since Grandpa has died she lives in a guesthouse. At afternoon tea time she plays the piano—I dance round the large room madly to the music. Everyone applauds. Afterwards she smokes a roll-your-own with her cup of tea while I sip pink lemonade. She tells me wonderful stories while we suck boiled lollies. Then she lets me try her clothes and jewellery on – they are gorgeous!

Chapter 12

"TU Y YO"

"His name is James and he is a famous American writer," one of my American friends tells me. "He just needs a couple of girls to go out with him tonight."

I suppose that Christine and I can't go too far wrong because there are two of us and only one of him, and the thought of a decent meal is always enticing. So we agree.

James turns out to be short, fat and decidedly on the unkempt side, certainly nothing to write home about in the looks department. No wonder he has to get someone else to line him up with girls. The consolation is that he knows his way around Madrid and takes us to a wonderful old restaurant called Casa Botin, just off the Plaza Mayor. It is where Hemingway and Michener used to eat, he tells us. I eat the *cochonillo asado* (roast suckling pig) which is wonderful, as is the décor—an 18th century building with beamed ceilings, hanging copper pots, tiled ovens and walls covered with memorabilia. It's the oldest restaurant in the world, James informs us.

James also turns out to be a very entertaining conversationalist, which consolidates my theory that unattractive people often have great personalities because they have to work hard on themselves. He has us both in constant fits of giggles.

After dinner, we grab a cab and head towards an even older and far seedier part of Madrid. We pull up outside a rundown building with a flashing neon sign advising that the name of the place is "Tu y Yo". Inside, it is dark and uninspiring with a lacklustre quartet playing in the far corner behind a small dance floor, which has a few couples sliding around it. Lined up along the front wall are about ten women, who have figure-hugging dresses on, with zippers down the front. "For easy access," James tells us. "They're prostitutes. Some of them have flats nearby, others will just hop in the back seat of a taxi and do their business while they drive around the block a few times."

Some of the men think we are in the same line of business and ask James, "*Cuanto cuesta?*" (How much do we cost?) What a strange juxtaposition exists in Madrid! On one hand Spain is such a seriously Catholic country, with church pews always filled, Saint days observed religiously, movies squeaky clean (always with even the most chaste kiss edited out), news and books censored, young girls always accompanied to ensure their virtue is protected to the nth degree and yet prostitutes operate openly. James, who has been very busy all night taking notes, is very gentlemanly in his behaviour towards us and hastily ushers us out of the club. He's one of the few men we have encountered that hasn't put the "hard word" on us. He seems to be happy just to squire us around.

I've heard there has been plenty of this type of activity in Sydney's Kings Cross since the Americans came to Australia on their R & R from the Vietnam War. I would certainly have to be down to the last card in the pack to work in that profession.

My other Grandma

Sometimes I visit my other grandmother after school. She's not like Grandma Alexander at all. Her house is as neat as a pin and smells delicious because there's always cake or biscuits cooking in the oven. But I don't like her toilet. It is in a shed out in the backyard and has fat white grubs in it. Mum tells me they're maggots. I never go to the toilet when I'm at Grandma's place. I hold on until I get home. Sometimes my tummy aches.

Chapter 13

UNAS AVENTURAS EN LA BASE AEREA AMERICANA

As Christina and I are walking up Calle de La Gasca late one afternoon, we discuss whether we are going to eat another helping of cornflakes for dinner, one of the main staples of our diet as neither of us are into cooking, or lash out on a *bocadillo*. Unexpectedly, we run into Harry and Charles, two guys from the air base at Torrejon I'd met at Peppi's shop.

"Where've you been? We've been back to the shop looking for you and wondered what happened. When we asked Peppi, he said you just left."

"In rather a hurry," I say and give them the lowdown.

They invite us for dinner out near the air base at the Long Horn Steakhouse Restaurant, which caters especially for Americans and serves enormous steaks and whole chickens, with mountains of chips. Although much more appealing than cornflakes, or for that matter the *bocadillo* we had in mind, I tell them that I like Spanish food much better. But Harry and Charles find this difficult to understand. "The helpings are way too small, and there's too much garlic. And no chips!" they plead. So in the end we agree. What can we do? They're paying.

After dinner they try to persuade us to go back to the air base with them, but I am more than a bit dubious about it, as we don't have the necessary pass.

"You won't believe what you can buy at the commissary on the base. All you have to do is just duck your heads down as we go through the security gate. We've done it heaps of times before without a problem," Harry says.

In the end, against my better judgment, we agree. Of course, no sooner do we go through the gate than a very loud siren screeches into the night right behind us. Several cars with lights flashing on their roofs surround us and force us to pull over. Uniformed men with rifles at the ready order us out of the car and steer us at gunpoint towards a block which has ADMINISTRATION written on the door. Then they hustle us down a long cement hallway to the commander's office.

My knees feel like they've disappeared and I feel like I'm going to throw up, as the Commander—all seriousness and glowering looks—barks at us, "You have breached United States Air Force security. May I see your identification papers?"

We both breathe a sigh of relief, because for once we both have our passports with us.

"I am going to have to come to a decision about whether to put you into the lock-up for the night. The lieutenant will show you where to wait while I consider what action we are going to take in the matter!"

We are shown into a small room with barred windows. Two armed guards stand at the door as we anxiously await our fate. After what seems like forever, we are shown back into the commander's office.

"I have decided to let you off the hook this time, but I want you girls to realise that you have done something extremely serious."

It is well after midnight when we are driven back to Madrid by the two poker-faced armed Air Force security guards.

We don't see Harry and Charles again. Nor do we dare to ask what happened to them.

Urghhhh!

Veggies look and taste yuk! Especially beans. Mum cooks them for so long they nearly melt, are almost grey and feel slimy in my mouth. I don't like beetroot either—the colour or the taste. And I really hate pineapple! It makes my teeth grind. Mum puts the pineapple in the Quikmix. Now it looks like puked up pineapple. She makes me stay at the table until I eat all of the above. It's not fair! Why do I have to eat things I don't like? When I grow up I'm not going to eat things I don't like and I'm going to drink lemonade all the time—not just at birthday parties.

Chapter 14

UN ENCUENTRO MUY EXTRANO

Once again Christina and I are between jobs. We have been working in a new nightclub in Calle de Lagasca in "public relations". All we've had to do is dance with the blokes who are working here until enough other people get up to dance. When the floor is crowded, the boss gives us the nod and we sit down. Unfortunately for us, our public relations have worked too well. The club has become so popular that people are dancing without any encouragement. They don't need us anymore!

While we are lamenting our fate over a *café con leche* at the café on the corner, we meet Paul, a friend of the club's owner. He tells us that there are some jobs going with a bloke called Jaime de Mora y Aragon, the Queen of Belgium's brother, he informs us importantly, in his nightclub, Salon des Artes, in Barcelona. We hope with such an illustrious relo he will be a reasonably safe bet. Anyway we don't have much of a choice. We hitchhike down the next day, arriving at the club in the late afternoon.

Jaime is playing the piano on a small, elevated platform at the front of the nightclub. When he stands up to greet us

I have to swallow my giggles. With his tall, slender build, slicked-back hair, long face with somewhat gaunt features, waxed moustache curled up at each side, monocle and cane, he is certainly not a run-of-the-mill Spaniard. He could in fact easily pass for Salvador Dali's brother. He invites us inside and offers us a drink.

Christina and I are wondering what we will be expected to do but before we can ask, Jaime volunteers that he is looking for hostesses. We are still not quite sure what this would involve, however, once our eyes adjust to the dim and dingy surroundings we see that there are a lot of dark, older men of Middle Eastern appearance drinking at the far end of the bar. Jaime leaves us to go and talk to them.

"He is telling them that we are two English virgins and is trying to sell us off to these men for three hundred cows," Christina, whose Spanish is a whole lot better than mine, whispers furtively.

Naturally this prospect does not appeal to us, but we decide that now is not the moment to try to make an escape. There are too many of them, and our luggage is hidden somewhere behind the reception counter. It is well after midnight when Jaime finally takes us to a very elegant, beautifully furnished apartment, where we are to sleep for the night. It is directly above his, he tells us. We take the precaution of tipping a chair under the door handle, in case we get any unexpected visitors during the night, especially from our would-be purchasers. We don't sleep at all. As soon as the first dawn light appears, we grab our things, race down the stairs past a surprised-looking *portero* and into the street.

Back in Madrid and still job-hunting, a few days later Christina and I answer an ad for English-speaking bar staff at an American bar, but after the job interview, neither of us is 100% *au fait* as to exactly what an American bar is, or for that matter, what the job entails. Still strapped for cash, we decide to turn up at six o'clock ready to work and play it from there. The customers, as it turns out, are mainly blokes from the American air base at Tarejon and English-speaking tourists. They are supposed to buy *us* drinks, as well as their own, so the bar makes double the money. We start to get a bit wary about our duties, particularly after we speak to some of the other girls, who intimate that we are expected to provide "other services".

When we tell the manager that we are leaving he wags his head from side to side while saying "*Non, non, senoritas*" then offers to pay us double if we stay. In our current dire financial situation this offer can't be sneezed at so we decide to hang in until one of the other girls tells us to watch it, because she's overheard the manager talking to the bar owner and they have us in mind for themselves. This time we don't hesitate and hightail it up the street, with the little plump Spanish manager, cigar in hand, smoke trailing behind him, in hot pursuit yelling "*Espera, espera!*" We are long gone by the time he has puffed his way to the end of the street.

Over the past few months, tennis has gone from taking the back seat to completely out the window but after these last couple of episodes on the job market, coaching tennis, which I've found tedious in the past, doesn't look so bad at all and tournaments would be a splendid proposition.

A Backyard Concert

I borrow Dad's typewriter to type out the invitations, then sweep up the garage and stack some old wooden crates together for the stage. The neighbours are surprised when they turn up. Old Miss Redfern from across the road says, "The invitation looked so professional." I dance and sing— I love performing. It's what I dream about doing when I grow up. It's hard to get me off the stage. Finally, Mum offers to make everyone a cup of tea.

Chapter 15

ESTAMOS DESESPERADOS

Things are really getting desperate in the finance department. Mum and Dad sent me some money to buy a car, but I've almost completely spent it on other things—mainly everyday expenses. To make matters worse, Christina doesn't have a brass razoo either and has been borrowing from me for the past few months. Mum and Dad will kill me if they find out. She told me that her family in England are very wealthy, but she can't get any money from them due to a law that does not allow more than thirty pounds to be sent out of the country per year. She promises faithfully to pay me back, just as soon as we get to England.

The two sisters have given us the flick from their apartment, so we've had to find one of our own. Fortunately, the car money from my parents arrived in the nick of time. However, the real estate agent charged us three months' rent as a letting fee, as well as requiring a month in advance. Now we have hardly enough money to feed ourselves, let alone to keep up the rent payments. The agent did suggest he'd be willing to accept sex in exchange for the rent but we declined. Not a difficult decision.

To add to our woes, the flat is very basic and the little furniture in it is miserable. The block is in a really rundown and suspect area. We are constantly being followed from the Metro station by small, grubby men with monumental body odour. They try to grab at us as we make our way to the flat, causing us to fumble with the keys at the door.

I am just about at my wits' end, when I receive a letter which has somehow managed to find its way from Dunlop's Sporting Goods office in England to the Real Madrid Club, inviting me to play in the spring circuit in the south of Italy during April. The first tournament is in Catania in Sicily starting in two weeks. What a lucky break! Although I've hardly been playing at all and am probably way down in my fitness level, if I squeeze in a bit of practice before I leave, that should do the trick. Bob Howe, the manager at Dunlop's has certainly gone over and above the call of duty the way he has been forwarding my mail to me, organising tournaments, and keeping up the supply of rackets and strings. None of us lower-ranking players have any contracts or formal agreements with either Dunlop's or the tournaments. It's all totally ad hoc and a major challenge to say the least.

At the last minute, Christina decides she will come with me because I plan to head back to England afterwards. She can't really afford to stay on in Madrid without any money. We have no alternative but to do a runner from the flat, leaving half our things behind. But I make sure I keep my rackets close at hand.

The day before we are to leave for Italy, after a practice session at the Real Madrid Club, Chistina and I have one last mosey around our favourite haunts in Madrid. We spend a wonderful day walking past the fabulous boutiques on

Calle de Serrano, checking out the sales at Gallerias Preciados and Cortes Ingles, then walking up and down the Gran Via several times, pausing to admire the Plazas de Colon and Cibeles and the marvellous winged creatures on top of the buildings. Thoroughly exhausted, in the late afternoon we end up at the Café Gijon, in the Paseo Recoletos. Although it is spring and the sky is piercingly blue and cloudless, there is no one sitting outside on the *terraza*, because an icy wind is blowing straight off the Sierra de Nevada. We head inside to sit among the writers, intellectuals and artists who have come to spend hours over a coffee, while they engage in their *tertulias*, (discussions) just like the famous literary characters of the past. And of course there are the tourists who, like us, come to the Café Gijon to people watch.

As I sip my *café con leche*, I try to be as surreptitious as possible while I check out all the fabulously dressed people engaged in animated, no doubt fascinating conversations. The noise level is deafening as everyone seems to be talking at the same time. Along one side of the café at the stand-up bar I notice two of the most gorgeous men I've ever seen in Madrid. They tower over the others gathered at the bar. They can't be from around here, I surmise.

At five foot nine, I am taller than the average Madrileno. These two gorgeous specimens of manhood are both over six feet. They must come from somewhere up north, like Senora del Puerto, who is much bigger than most of the other Madrilenas. The taller one, who has light hair and blue eyes, is casually dressed. The other, who is not quite as tall, has black hair, dark flashing eyes and the most amazing smile. He is impeccably dressed in the most beautiful dark suit and is the type of man I dream about falling in love with. As I look around the room, I notice I am not the only woman who feels like that.

I can't help wondering who he is, where he comes from and what kind of work he does. He certainly doesn't look like he sits in an office. He looks more like one of the jetsetters I saw in Monte Carlo where I played my first overseas tournament. Or maybe he is a film star, or even royalty.

"Definitely not royalty," Christina says. "He's much too handsome for that!"

I have to laugh. Unfortunately, as we are leaving the next day, I'll never find out.

The Marks System

Mum has started a new system for our pocket money. We have to earn it now, she says, not just get it like we did before. It will teach us to appreciate the "value of money," she tells us. It's called the Marks System. Each job is worth ten marks. Mum has stuck a big piece of cardboard on the wall above the fridge with our names on it and every time we do a task, she puts down our marks—ten for each job. When we get a hundred marks we get two shillings. It's slave labour, if you ask me. I like the old system much better.

Chapter 16

ADIOS ESPANA!

Due to our lack of funds we decide to hitchhike. It is early evening when Christina and I finally arrive at the Spanish border, where the guards try to flirt madly with us—without success. They then take great delight in making us open our suitcases. Needless to say, they are sorely disappointed when confronted with the contents of *my* suitcase—then horrified when their nostrils are assailed with the smell of my dirty sweaty sandshoes, socks and tennis clothes from my last minute practice, which as usual, are in a plastic bag right at the top of my case. Totally disgusted, they move briskly on to our documentation, and after a careful examination of our passports, we are at last allowed through.

We drag our bags and my rackets a short way down the street, then as it is getting dark, plonk ourselves down for the night on a couple of stone benches. It is too late to go any further. And anyway we are buggered! I am also starving so I furrow in my handbag for my unfinished *bocadillo* from lunch, which by this stage is looking a bit the worse for wear. The chorizo has become slimy and slides out the side of my roll. The manchego cheese, which must have melted in the hot sun earlier in the day, is now runny. It doesn't look at all appetising, but it is all I have. I don't even have a drink to wash it down with.

As soon as it becomes dark, we lie down and try to sleep. It is difficult. Car lights continuously flash in our faces and the bench is so narrow I nearly fall off every time I try to turn over. I am also scared. I hardly sleep at all. The bench becomes harder and harder as the night wears on, and in the early hours of the morning, I freeze. I am relieved when at last dawn arrives and I can finally quit the most uncomfortable bed I've ever slept on. When I stand up, I can feel every bone in my body and none of them are happy. I certainly hope that I won't ever have to sleep like this again.

We are extremely lucky to get to Catania, the venue of the first tournament, in one piece. Hitchhiking turns out to be a nightmare! I lose count of how many times we have to grab our bags and make quick escapes out of cars and trucks. Halfway across France, a driver takes us right off the main road for several miles and threatens to hit us with an empty wine bottle if we don't have sex with him, which he explains with a series of actions and whistles. When he doesn't meet with success, he dumps us and our bags on the side of the road and drives off in a huff, leaving us miles from anywhere. We lug our bags back up the hill, where fortunately we manage to get a lift with some nice English people for a change.

Unfortunately, they are only going to the north of Italy. Once again we have to look for another lift. This time we get a ride with a randy Italian truck driver, who can't keep his hands to himself. We take it in turns to sleep, while one of us remains on guard, both of us keeping our hands on our bag handles, ready to jump, even in our sleep.

After several more lecherous Italian truck drivers, we finally arrive at the dock at the bottom of Calabria and catch the ferry to Sicily. We sigh with relief when we finally make it on board, then bump our way across the sea to Catania. On shore it takes us a while to get our land legs. We are also still feeling decidedly seedy from lack of sleep over the last couple of days.

Without any warning, as we pass a large bush, a man jumps out with his pants hanging down to his knees, pulling at the contents of his trousers.

"He's masturbating," says Christina, who is much more knowledgeable about this type of thing, as she digs me in the side with her elbow.

I am shocked, as I have never seen a man in the nude before, except for those long-ago baths with my brother John and that brief display of my tennis coach's appendage. But in the full light of day, this sweaty grunting man is not a pretty sight. We look the other way, then at each other, and keep walking until we get around the corner. There, much to the amazement of the passers-by, we fall onto the grass verge, bursting into fits of uncontrollable giggles.

It is funny to begin with but by the end of our first day in Catania, this kind of behaviour is starting to wear a bit thin. Some of the men try to pinch our bottoms, grope at our crotches and grab at our breasts, not to mention several other masturbators, leaping out from behind bushes, pants down, confronting us with their wares. We are soon past laughing. It is beyond me what they hope to achieve with these antics. Surely they have never had any success with women, using this method!

As we make our way down the footpath of a wide, tree-lined boulevard towards the centre of town, the snow-capped peak of Mount Etna peeks between the buildings at the far side of the town *piazza*. The main buildings on the square are stunning. Statues of angels cling to their sides, the sculpture of an elephant sits atop a pole and an old lady dressed in black, head bowed, kneels at the bottom of the ancient town hall stairwell, with a note asking for money. She is the only woman we see all day. When we finally arrive at the accommodation the tournament has arranged for us in a hotel near the club, we flop onto the bed, so absolutely dead tired that we sleep right through until morning, not even waking to eat dinner!

The next morning, I make the mistake of walking down to the tennis club in my tennis skirt. By the time I arrive, I find that I have attracted a retinue of about twenty short dark Italians who are following me close behind, trying to touch me up. I swing my racket towards them while sprouting my Italian version of "piss off". *"Andare all'inferno. Solo perche tua madre e una prostituta non e necesario che tutte le regazze sono cosi"*. (Go to hell. Because your mother is a prostitute it's not necesary that all girls are like that).

Fortunately, they do not have the money to come into the club to watch the tournament so I am safe once inside the gate. But I leave behind such a furore outside, that the tournament director comes out and starts waving his arms and shouting at the men, and then at me.

"You must wear your track pants when you are going back and forth to the hotel in future," he instructs.

I win my first match easily then can't resist heading down to the beach for a swim. But that too proves to be a mistake! No sooner do I step on the sand, than I am immediately surrounded by more small dark men who seem to appear out of nowhere. When I look around I notice that there aren't any other women on the beach so I take a deep breath then run for it, my well-practised long strides leaving the Sicilians behind in no time at all.

I lose in the finals but it is a very good result considering that I haven't been playing much over the past couple of months. However, when I go to the office to collect my expenses for the week, the president tries to fob me off.

"You can collect your money in Roma," he tells me.

The other girls have already warned me that I have to make sure I get my money straightaway, otherwise I won't get paid. Anyway I won't have the money to pay for the hotel if I don't. So I stand firm.

"You agreed to pay me $100 for the week and I need the money now," I insist, and sit down ready to wait it out.

Somewhat reluctantly, he opens his drawer and passes me an envelope. The early business training I received with Dad collecting the rents has stood me in good stead on this particular occasion.

I play tournaments in Palermo—where I run in to my brother, John, and the Australian team, Reggio Calabria, Napoli, and then Rome, which I instantly fall in love with. I would dearly love to stay longer and explore, but I can't afford it. As soon as I lose, Christina and I head for England.

We disembark at Dover, feeling decidedly seedy after a rocky trip over the English Channel in very bleak conditions. From the moment we get on the train, the weather deteriorates even more. The sky is now a solid block of grey cloud, with not a speck of blue, and it doesn't stop raining the whole trip. I am beginning to feel miserable already. As the train clickety-clacks its way through lush green fields and small villages *en route* to London, depressing thoughts of endless rain and grey skies fill my mind. Even the laundry is hanging dispiritedly in pocket handkerchief backyards behind ancient blocks of flats. Buckley's chance of getting dry!

It is all hustle and bustle when we arrive at Victoria Station, dead buggered and decidedly grimy. Before Christina leaves to catch the train home, she carefully writes down the address of Dunlop's office and swears blind that as soon as she gets to her parents' place, she will send the money she owes me.

Needless to say I never see her—or my money—again!

I'm so exhausted I can't bear the thought of dragging my bags another inch, so I hop in a taxi and ask the driver to take me to a cheap bed and breakfast in the area. I have to go to Dunlop's the next day to pick up my new rackets and mail. It's in Piccadilly, only about a mile away, so I'll be able to walk.

I wonder what's Inside?

Mum comes home with one of those brown paper packets again. She won't tell me what's in it. She puts it in the divan drawer. While she's in the shower, I open the drawer and get it out. I shake it. I press it. I can't open the packet because it's all stuck down with sticky tape. Mum will know I've fiddled with it. I ask my sister what's in it. "Modess," she says. "When you're 13 you'll get your periods. That's what they're for. I'm still none the wiser. But I don't want to get my periods whatever they are."

Chapter 17

THE GARDEN PARTY AT THE HURLINGHAM CLUB

I've played in the middle of the night in Bathurst, with ice on the side of the court in Cowra and in such unbelievable heat in Brisbane that it took me nearly a month to recover from dehydration, but the spring circuit tournaments leading up to Wimbledon take the cake. Rain, rain and then more rain and sometimes even snow!

Bob Howe, the manager of Dunlop's in London has told me that I have to play in these tournaments because I need to beat as many English girls as possible in order to get into the Wimbledon draw. There are no computer rankings. To play in Wimbledon is every Australian tennis player's (and even more so, generally speaking, their parents') dream. For me it means getting 50 English pounds in my pocket, my meals every day, heaps of Fred Perry gear, tickets to watch the tournament, as well as being picked up in a Rolls while I am still in the tournament. Now *that* isn't something to be sneezed at, although in retrospect I probably would have been better off playing in Junior Wimbledon, which that year was won by Judy Salome, the gorgeous Dutch girl I'd beaten in the finals at Monte Carlo.

So what's a girl to do? I put my nose down and bum up, enduring match after match in very dreary, wet, miserable conditions on soggy loam courts in the five run-up tournaments before Wimbledon and obviously manage to beat enough English girls, because I make the draw! As I'm travelling by myself, Bob arranges for me to be billeted with families, which at least gives me some company, home cooking and comforts. Cheap bed-and-breakfasts are lonely places. The only money I receive are the train fares between tournaments calculated to the last penny which are funded by the tennis clubs as are the lunches—generally ploughman's lunches comprising micro-thin pieces of cheese, cucumber and tomato, which hardly satisfy my hearty tennis player's appetite. By afternoon tea time I'm ravenous and tuck into way too much of all the wrong things.

Everyone has told me about the fabulous garden party prior to Wimbledon, held in the grounds of the very exclusive Hurlingham club, a magnificent 42-acre cocoon of green lawns and magnificently landscaped gardens overlooking the Thames. The membership comprises the titled and very wealthy Londoners. I am particularly excited because for the first time this year, Fred Perry is going to compete with Teddy Tinling in the fashion stakes. While Fred is known for his "no nonsense" pleated skirts and plain cotton shirts (relieved only by his famous logo) the very eccentric Teddy Tinling is the reigning king of exotic tennis wear. His designs are renowned for making the top players look more like tutu-ed ballerinas doing a *pas de deux* than serious competitors in a tennis match! Although I would have preferred to be one of Teddy's girls, I've been chosen to be Fred's model.

Unfortunately, when the big day arrives, the English weather stays true to form. Italian Lea Pericola and I are greeted by sodden flower beds. Hyacinths and sarcococcas bend to the wind; both their sweet perfume and us are drowned by the buckets of rain which pour down non-stop all day. So instead of strutting our stuff as has been planned, Lea and I have our photos taken running across sodden grass and jumping puddles while the deluge continues.

Lea—modelling for Teddy—is renowned at Wimbledon for 'swirling to defeat' in a scalloped A-line dress, showing lace-trimmed panties and a pink rayon petticoat every time she served. She is also known for her elaborate beehive hairstyles, and is particularly miffed having spent most of the morning in heated rollers. After only a minute in the rain, her beautiful hairstyle is a soggy mess.

Still, I can't help feeling I've had a lucky break, because the outfit Fred Perry has designed for me is an absolute shocker. Instead of a skirt, it is all in one piece, a bit like a jumpsuit except that the bottom part is like bloomers. They have obviously been inspired by those daring lace panties worn by Gussy Moran back in the late 40s which were designed by Teddy Tinling, and caused such a furore that poor old Teddy was asked to "take leave from" his position as Player Liaison, which he'd held at Wimbledon for years.

The only good part of the day is when the weather eventually clears later in the afternoon. We are invited to sit down to a very elegant silver-service afternoon tea on the lawns outside the club house while an impeccably uniformed military band marches up and down playing stirring music. There are no pikelets, jam and cream like we usually have with our afternoon tea at home. Instead we are served the thinnest cucumber sandwiches I've ever eaten (not that I've had too many), which just melt in my mouth. They are washed down with thimblefuls of tea in dainty china cups.

Playing doctors

Mum and Dad give me a doctor's kit for my birthday. I love it. I can hardly wait to start playing doctors. When my cousin comes over, we go into my bedroom. I get her to lie on the bed. She is the patient. I am the doctor. I listen to her heart with my stethoscope, then I get her to pull down her pants and am just about to give her a needle in the bottom, like Dr Rosati does, when mum comes in. She snatches the needle and plonks it back in the kit-box. We never get to play together again. I don't ever see the doctor's kit again either.

Chapter 18

WIMBLEDON

On the day of my first match at Wimbledon, a chauffeur in full livery, complete with cap, arrives in a black, shiny Rolls Royce at the boarding house in Putney where I am staying. The other not so fortunate players who haven't made the draw, plus our landlady dressed in a crinoline brunch coat with her hair in rollers, covered by a paisley chiffon scarf, gather at the front door to wave me goodbye. I hop in the front with the driver because I get carsick in the back and am so excited that I don't shut up the whole trip! As we drive regally along, everyone keeps turning around, to see if they recognise me. "Am I someone famous?"

The sun, for once, is shining as we drive into the club grounds past mile-long queues of people waiting for tickets for the standing room area. Loud, spruiking scalpers are plying the crowd with tickets at exorbitant prices. The crowd parts as we drive through the gates then pass the centre court to the players' change room. Autograph seekers thrust their books at me as I get out. I sign a few, and then race for the cover of the Ladies. No doubt they will be disappointed when they find out that I am not one of the top players.

I am due to play Margaret Court, the number one seed, in the singles in the first round at 11am, and try to cool my nerves before the match. I am very relieved that, due to rain, we have been rescheduled to play on court 17. It would have been a nightmare to play her on the centre court, where we were originally drawn.

As I make my way through the crowds milling around the outside courts, adrenalin surges through my body, making my knees go weak. Unfortunately, I've managed to get very little practice on grass since I've been in England, and find the transition from the very slow loam courts I've been playing on to the faster-than-lightning grass difficult. The long, lush, English grass is also very different from the Australian lawn courts which bake themselves corn-coloured during our long hot summers, by the end of which there is mostly dirt with only a few odd spikes of grass around the service line.

There is a large crowd crammed around the court, which I am not used to. I become caught up in the occasion. Margaret Court turns out to be every bit as formidable an opponent as I imagined she would be. As well as being the number one seed in the tournament, she is the current Australian champion. It doesn't help that grass is her favourite surface and really suits her serve/volley game to a tee. I play in a hesitant manner, mistime the ball and don't really settle down in the match at all. It is not a pleasant experience.

I already had the "nervous Nellies" before the match, having read a feature in the paper in the morning, which compared the various arm lengths of the players in this year's tournament. I am especially intimidated by the fact that Margaret's arm length is longer than that of two thirds of the players in the men's draw. That doesn't help my confidence and whenever she comes into the net during the match, it's all I can think about. My worst fears are confirmed. It is just impossible to get the ball past her. It feels like she is all over the place without taking more than a step in any direction. The reality: with that massive arm stretch extended to the maximum, she is!

Margaret also hits the ball with a lot more power and depth than I am used to, which I've heard is due to the fact that Frank Sedgman (who is coaching her) has had her doing weight training. She wins easily but fortunately I manage to get a game in the second set, for which I get a big cheer from the crowd. 6–love, 6–love would be very embarrassing even though she is the number one seed and we are on an outside court.

I did expect to lose so I am not that disappointed. As I walk back to the change rooms by the other outside courts I notice that there are a lot of very good players. As only 128 players make the draw, I feel I've done well just to get into the tournament, especially when I take into consideration that I am far from dedicated, have a dreadful second serve and a volatile temperament—indeed the female version of McEnroe. I have also smoked all the cigarettes that the Rothman and Malboro (tournament sponsors at that time) representatives gave me to hand around to the spectators. Besides, Margaret has the advantage of an entourage, whereas I am here all by myself. And I'm only 18.

I console myself in the change room with a long hot shower followed by afternoon tea on the lawn in the sun outside the centre court. I eat the biggest, sweetest strawberries I've ever tasted, with lashings of cream, washed down with a halfway decent cup of tea. I've never really liked strawberries all that much before, having always found them a bit sour, but these English ones are so sweet and luscious. They are truly to die for!

On the middle Saturday of the tournament, my brother, John, and I are set down to play on the centre court against Margaret Court and Marty Reissen. John is touring in the Davis Cup team managed by Harry Hopman and this is the first time we've played at the same tournament since Palermo.

Although we are the next match on, and have been duly instructed where to wait, I am the only one who is sitting on the hard, board seats in the small room behind the centre court. The other more experienced players and my brother, who no doubt has been counselled by Harry Hopman, remain in the comfort of the change rooms until the very last moment. Unfortunately this gives me too much time for my already shattered nerves to kick in, especially as right above the doorway leading out to the centre court are the lines from Rudyard Kipling's poem:

"If you can meet with Triumph and Disaster
And treat those two impostors just the same."

Triumph I can handle easily. It is Disaster that is my main concern.

I find it hard to believe that I am about to play on the hallowed Wimbledon turf, the scene of so many long and torrid battles fought by past champions. As a young girl growing up, I dreamt of this moment, as I'd lain sprawled on my parents' bed, sipping hot, sweet tea and listening to crackly radio broadcasts from Wimbledon in the early hours of the morning. Now I am here and it is about to happen.

When the others arrive and I stand up to go out on the court, I can't feel my knees. They've completely gone to jelly. Nor, as hard as I try, can I get the butterflies in my stomach to fly in formation. They are running wild. I make the mistake of looking up at the stands, which are full to overflowing with people. They shimmer in the afternoon sun, appearing to rise out of the ground, almost perpendicularly. I pray fervently to the god of all tennis players that I will play my best, not let my partner down, or worst of all make a fool of myself. I step gingerly forward, desperately wishing that I was a turtle and could just disappear into my shell.

John advises me to lob every ball and the tactic works. We lose but only just. The good part is that as only the third brother and sister combination in the history of Wimbledon we are the underdogs and thus the crowd favourites. We are cheered loudly every time we win a point. Mum will certainly be very proud and happy as it has always been her dream for John and me to play mixed doubles on the centre court at Wimbledon.

I love cuddles

But Mummy doesn't. Not now I'm a big girl she says. I'm too old for them. But Daddy still loves them. Every night I squeeze into his chair while he watches the news and get lots of cuddles. Mummy tells me not to annoy Daddy. She says he's tired. He's been working hard all day and doesn't like me crawling all over him. No more cuddles. Except for my teddy bear and Snow Boots.

Chapter 19

SANTANDER, SAN SEBASTIAN, BILBAO AND OVIEDO

After Wimbledon, I play in tournaments at St Annes on Lytham, Wolverhampton (where it rains all week) and at the Priory Club in Birmingham (where I eat the most wonderful Indian food every night), before heading off to Wengen in Switzerland then on to the north of Spain.

I am surprised when I arrive in Santander. I've always imagined Spanish regional towns to be like the dry, dusty *pueblos* I've seen in the movies. But Santander turns out to be nothing like that at all. It is in fact a very pretty little fishing village situated on a bay, surrounded by lush greenery with mountains behind it. When I sit on the terrace in front of the club house, which is located across the road from the water, I can see brightly coloured boats bobbing up and down, and fire-engine red life buoys affixed to the wooden support posts of the wharf.

While I was playing in the tournament at Wolverhampton, the Spanish players told me that if I just turned up here, they would let me play in the tournament. So that's what I've done. And fortunately, they are right. On my arrival when I meet with the officials of the Real Sociedad de Tenis de Magdalena, they are delighted to extend an invitation to both my partner Terese Mackay and me to play in the Santander tournament, as well as in another three tournaments afterwards. The president then insists on showing me a whole pile of letters from other players "en Englees". "Mi non speakie Englees," he then tells me, wagging his finger at me then giving his shoulders a quick shrug.

What a relief! I would hate to have to go back to dreary, wet old England. My tail would definitely be between my legs.

When I look at the women's draw, I see it is going to be pretty easy-going this week as there are only eight women in the tournament. And except for my partner and me, the others are all Spanish and not very strong players. At this time in Spain there aren't a lot of women tennis players. In fact, it isn't the custom for Spanish women to play sport at all.

We manage to find a small *pensione*, just a short walk up the road from the tennis club, which is cheap and clean. The only drawback is that it has a peculiar mouldy plumbing smell. But I don't mind. I love being in Spain, even though the weather is not as hot and sunny as I'd hoped it would be. In fact, it has rained quite a bit and is windy, but it is nowhere near as bad as England, and the smell of the salt water wafting across the road is compensation enough. It reminds me of our home in Narrabeen when the north easterly blows.

There are other benefits. Spanish men are gorgeous. Their dark skin and hair, soulful eyes, mysterious broody temperaments and very different line of chat, certainly make them a lot more interesting than the boys back home on the Northern Beaches. I have also fallen in love with garlic.

I win the tournament in Santander playing against Ana Maria Estelella, the reigning Spanish champion in the final.

She must surely be very pissed off that I've turned up, as she no doubt usually wins these tournaments hands down. Terese and I win the doubles.

The next tournament is in San Sebastian, a much bigger town than Santander. I am instantly enchanted by it, especially the old part. Wandering down the narrow, cobbled streets makes me feel like I am living in another era. So, while Terese is busy lighting candles at every church for the drought to break at her family property in her hometown Wellington (a town in inland NSW located at the junction of the Macquarie and Bell Rivers), I take the opportunity to explore. I much prefer to socialise and see the sights between matches than hang around at the tennis club. I don't even dream of practising when I have time off. It really wasn't until Navratilova burst on the scene in the mid-seventies that brought athleticism in tennis to a whole new level. Martina utilised cross training in the gym and played basketball under Nancy Lieberman (a former U.S. basketball champion and coach) to improve her fitness and toughen her mental approach, and had long practice sessions before matches. I definitely don't want to hit up too much before matches as I might do my run in the paddock.

And so I eat lunches at long trestle tables in dark, old restaurants with high beamed ceilings, overlooking the bay. I sit alongside weathered Basque fishermen and watch them demolish huge helpings of food, washing it down with large gulps from litre bottles of red wine. My favourite dish, I decide after considerable contemplation, is *Lomo de Bacalao en salsa de tomate*, which is a moist, white fish simmering in lots of rich garlic and tomato sauce. The fish is salted cod but it tastes nothing like the salted fish Mum sometimes made 'for a change'—that was always dry, flaky and very salty, even though she soaked it in milk beforehand. And it is certainly much better than the battered fish and greasy chips that we sometimes had on a Friday night when Mum "wanted a rest" from cooking.

I notice that Spanish manners are also very different. At home, dunking and mopping up sauce with bread are definitely big no-nos and in fact considered very bad manners, but here everyone does it! I don't miss an opportunity to mop up the sauce with crusty bread, which is so delicious it would be a crime to leave it.

Bilbao, the venue of the next tournament, is an industrial port city with a big tennis club. Again I win the singles against Ana Maria Estelella, who no doubt by now really has the poops with me. I win the doubles with Terese, and the mixed doubles with Maximo di Diminico. Unfortunately, the tournament winners still receive silver cups at the Spanish tournaments and I now have nine huge cups to drag around with me.

The last tournament is in Oviedo, the capital of Asturias, a city of beautiful gardens, lots of interesting sculptures and many wonderful old buildings, as well as more ancient churches than you can poke a stick at, which serves to keep Terese happy. However, I certainly don't get a very warm welcome. On the way back to the hotel from the club on my first day, I am pursued by a group of black-clad women who throw stones and shout "Puta, puta, puta" loudly at me. My heart beats wildly as I run down the street as fast as I can, somewhat encumbered by my large tennis bag and rackets, with these old ducks following in hot pursuit. They appear to be gaining ground, despite the impediment of their nearly floor-length garb. I just manage to make it up the hotel steps and into the vestibule ahead of them, then past a very surprised looking concierge and into the lift. Phew!

I find out later that Oviedo is a very religious city. It is on el Camino de Santiago de Compostela, a road along which people make religious pilgrimages. Apparently, my tennis skirt is much too short. By dressing so indecently, I will no doubt lead the local men up the garden path and probably entice them behind the bushes too.

Apart from religion, the other serious pastime in Oviedo is drinking apple cider. The locals drink it everywhere and at all times of the day. One night, a group of us tennis players go to El Pigea in the Calle Gascona, a cobbled pedestrian road outside of the old town, lined with *chigres* (cider bars). The cider is really delicious, but the locals certainly have some very strange rituals. Cider pouring is considered an art form and the waiters take great pride in it. They hold the bottle high over their head with one of their arms fully extended and pour the cider straight over their shoulder into glasses that are held in their other arm. This is supposed to aerate the cider. As this ritual is required to be performed while looking straight ahead through the stream of liquid, half the cider sprays over the floor, leaving only a couple of mouthfuls in the glass. Custom dictates that you must gulp straight down whatever the waiter offers you, leaving a small amount in the bottom of the glass. As the glasses are shared, you have to then swirl the leftover cider around the glass to clean it out, and tip it on the floor before passing the glass to the next drinker.

Between the pouring and the tipping out, cider drinking certainly is a messy business. We end up sloshing around in a couple of inches of cider mixed with the sawdust which covers the floor, cigarette butts and rubbish. The Spanish, it seems, don't worry about putting their cigarettes out in ashtrays or their rubbish in the bins.

I really love being back in Spain, although the late meal times take a bit of getting used to. At home we usually ate dinner at six so Mum and Dad could watch the Channel 2 news at 7pm, but as most of the tennis is played in Spain from 5pm onwards, sometimes it is midnight before we sit down for dinner. The good news is that I don't have to get up in the morning until late. There is no Dad waking me up at the crack of dawn with fresh orange juice and a cup of tea, although I would do anything for a decent bloody cup of tea. In Spain, the best I've been able to get so far has been a stale tea bag dangling in tepid water, served with hot milk. I've had to resort to drinking *café con leche* instead.

I once again beat Anna Maria Estelella in the final of the singles, and later that day, Terese and I win the doubles against Anna Maria and Carmen Bustamente.

As Terese and I make our way to the station in Oviedo, laden down with a bag full of trophies, I am full of many fond memories of all the yummy things I have been eating—the buttery *toastadas con marmelada de albaricoque*, (toast and apricot jam), *merluza* (hake) in garlicky tomato sauce and not to mention the crunchy bread. We purchase our third-class tickets to Madrid, then head towards the platform, dragging our bags, tennis rackets and an old holdall, which one of the other players donated to us at the last minute. It is stuffed with the cups we've won over the past month. I tried to sell them at a pawn shop but the silver content was apparently negligible. However I did manage to offload one huge monster of a cup which didn't have *Women's* Champion on it to my Italian mixed partner for a couple of hundred pesetas.

The train is about to leave and we are still only at the beginning of the platform. Worse still, the third-class carriages are at the far end of the train. I can't manage my clothes bag, my rackets and the cups. Something's got to give. I ditch the holdall with all the cups in it and make a run for it, only just getting into the carriage before the train chugs out of the station. If only, I wish, the tournaments gave us money, it would make our lives a lot easier. Once inside, we find all the seats are taken and there is standing room only. We are packed in like sardines and would never have been able to manage with the cups as well.

At the last minute, as usual, we have had to bundle all our dirty tennis clothes into plastic bags and stick them in the top of our suitcases, so when a handsome Spaniard offers to put our luggage and rackets up on the rack, I am horrified. I pray he won't smell anything. But he nearly knocks me for six when he raises his arms—the smell of garlic and sweaty armpits is so strong. I am reassured that he won't smell a thing. By now it is 10pm and we are both exhausted, having played a full day's tennis. We are dead on our feet. As the train rattles on into the night, we drift off to sleep standing up, pinned tightly in place between the carriage wall and the other passengers. Fortunately, none of them take advantage of the situation.

After a couple of hours, we are all nearly thrown off our feet when the driver slams on the brakes and the train pulls up suddenly. We are shocked into wakefulness and it takes me a few moments to orient myself. The windows of our carriage are thrown open and hawkers selling bocadillos and drinks on trolleys are going up and down the platform. We ravenously hoe into a late supper of *bocadillo de jamon y cieso* (ham and cheese roll) washed down with strong, tepid coffee. As the train chugs out of the station, our stomachs no longer rumbling, we drift back to sleep once again and only wake up when the first morning light beams in through the carriage window.

My eyes are bleary and my whole body feels like hell. Fortunately, there are no mirrors around because I would hate to think what I look like. And thank goodness we haven't arranged for anyone to meet us. My reputation would be in tatters!

Murphy's Law. As I step off the train I nearly collide with the handsome guy I'd previously seen at the Café Gijon. I can't believe it! The most beautiful man in Madrid, who I never dreamt I would ever see again. And here I am, looking like the wreck of the *Hesperus*. My stomach drops, my heart beats wildly. But he just looks straight through me and keeps on walking, which isn't at all surprising really. After all, he doesn't know me from a bar of soap, and let's face it, no one would be interested in me at the moment, looking so disreputable. Let alone a gorgeous creature like him.

The old fig tree

The trunk is solid and hard underneath me. It's a struggle to get up to the top of the fig tree, but it's worth it. Here I am in my own world. I love this quiet space, this time alone when I do not have to rush back and forward across the tennis court, feel the anger involved when I lose a point to my brother or one of the neighbourhood boys, miss shots I think I shouldn't or feel the frustration of not hitting the ball as well as I would like. I can think my thoughts, let my mind wander and daydream to my heart's content.

Chapter 20

UNA CORRIDA DE TOROS

Terese is an Aussie country girl at heart and being away from home for so long is getting too much for her. She's missing her family and friends desperately. The train trip is the final straw. She longs for home comforts. That very afternoon she books her ticket back to Australia. But there is one thing she really wants to do before she leaves Madrid, and that is to go to a bullfight.

I haven't ever thought about going to a bullfight myself. I have a soft heart when it comes to animals. As a small child I'd decided to give up eating lamb and beef after Mum told me that the sweet little lambs gambolling in the fields and the soft-eyed calves we saw beside the road when we were holidaying in the country would shortly become our lamb chops or steaks for dinner. I couldn't believe it. And still find it hard to.

I'd also heard bullfighting is a cruel sport. But Terese is determined. George and Bill, two American friends of ours, come up trumps and offer to take us. They have some spare tickets given to them by a friend in the American Embassy in

Madrid because this afternoon, an American bullfighter, John Fulton, is going to make his debut professional bullfight. Although it is mid-autumn, it is a very hot steamy afternoon as we join the excited and colourful throng of *aficionados* making their way into the Plaza de Toros de Las Ventas, Spain's largest bullring. I love buildings and Las Ventas is worth seeing for its magnificent architecture alone. "*Neomudejar*, a combination of Spanish style with Islamic influence," George tells me.

We have excellent seats in the *delanteras*, only three rows back from the ring, fortunately on the shady side. The afternoon's proceedings begin with a band playing stirring, high spirited bullfighting songs called *Paso Dobles*, which arouse the emotions of the already excited crowd, entice children to dance, men to strut proudly back and forth, and me to tap my feet and click my fingers. When the gates swing open, a parade of horses and matadors in their colourful costumes makes its way around the ring. The atmosphere is electric as the drama is about to unfold.

Trumpets blare as the first matador makes his way into the ring. Then the bull is ushered out of the enclosure where he is being kept, appearing to be somewhat disoriented on his arrival. This isn't at all surprising with a crowd of nearly 25,000 people yelling for his blood. After being prodded by the picadors near the entrance, the bull keeps trying to rush at the horses and gore them under the saddle. I have to look away. Finally, the matador manages to attract the bull's attention by waving his red cape. Bill tells me that as bulls are colour blind it is the movement of the cape, not the colour that attracts the bull. Despite the initial lack of cooperation from the bull, the matador eventually succeeds in luring him to participate in the *corrida*. He goes on to make an elegant, accomplished display, sidestepping away from the cape, miraculously managing to remain unscathed as the bull charges past him.

A chorus of "Ole"s greets each successful *veronica*. Then the matador waves his cape to once more attract the bull's attention and proceeds with another successful pass. The crowd, many of whom have been throwing down cognacs most of the afternoon, loudly egg him on. The bullfighter, encouraged by the roars of the crowd, continues his dangerous dance, becoming more daring by the minute. He kneels, he feigns and sometimes he even turns his back on the bull. I hold my breath. By this stage the crowd is on its feet, aroused to a frenzy, shouting "Ole".

Blood is pouring out of the bull where the picadors have wounded it on his way into the ring, and where the *bandilleras* have stuck in their picks. Wild-eyed, it turns to make another charge. I put my hands over my eyes. I just can't bear to look anymore. It is becoming too gruesome for words. I glaze over and started dreaming about the handsome stranger at the railway station, his gleaming skin and shining, thick wavy hair. I've seen him twice now. But George nudges me out of my reverie because the bull is about to be killed. It is a rude awakening. The matador, with a sword in one hand and the cape in the other, enters into the ring alone. I can see the poor creature is on its last legs, having lost a significant amount of blood. It appears totally exhausted as it makes its last desperate charge. The matador uses his cape to attract the bull in a series of passes, both demonstrating his control over it and risking his life by getting especially close to it. Finally, he comes in for the kill, fortunately nailing it on the first go. For his clean kill, he is rewarded with the ear of the bull which is duly cut off and given to him. The matador then proudly strides around the ring and presents it to his *novia* (girlfriend).

When the American, John Fulton, comes into the ring for the last fight of the day, it's a different kettle of fish. Fulton appears nervous and unsure.

"The crowd would normally give a bullfighter a hard time for this type of clumsy performance," George tells me. "But I think they are being generous because he's an American."

The audience almost appears to be holding its collective breath as the fight gets underway. Fulton doesn't go in for as many smart manoeuvres as the previous bloke. In the end, somehow, he manages to kill the bull in one go although not cleanly enough to be awarded the ear. This is a big relief, because a rumour has been circulating that John Fulton was going to throw the ear towards the group of Americans where we are sitting. I was getting ready to duck.

I will never go to another bullfight after this one. But Terese is ecstatic. She is laughing, her eyes are shining. All the way home she tells me how she has really enjoyed every minute and it is something she'll never forget. Maybe she didn't find it so bloodthirsty because she is a country cousin. I shudder. It was definitely not my cup of tea. Although I have to admit it was a wonderful spectacle, the matadors are extremely handsome, and look very dashing dressed in their glittering, tightly fitted outfits that accentuate their slender waists and beautifully shaped bottoms.

I don't hear from Terese again after she gets home but find out later that she married a farmer and is living in Narromine. And she did go to another bullfight some years later.

It's a difficult decision

I'm trying to decide whether to be a doctor or a ballerina when I grow up. I do like the uniforms doctors wear—their white coats with their stethoscopes around their necks make them look very important. But ballerinas get to wear beautiful costumes and they also get lots of claps. I love applause. It's a hard decision. Mum says it would be a waste of time to study medicine. I'll end up getting married and having children. And anyway, she says, I don't like blood or needles. She certainly gives a career in medicine the kybosh.

Chapter 21

MAD MIKE

I'm now travelling with Sandie Walsham. Dad has arranged for us to play together. He thinks Sandie will be a steadying influence on me as she is four years older. We hit it off immediately when we discover that we both smoke.

We've competed in the English Spring Circuit, played at Wimbledon, then in Roosendaal in Holland where I met a Yugoslavian player, Boris, who arranges for us to play an exhibition in Ljubljana. Mike, a South African, who is definitely nothing to write home about in the tennis department, muscles in on the deal by offering to give us a lift there and back. It doesn't take us long to realise that he is not much of a driver either. On the way to Ljubljana he is very average, but on the way back he is practically incapable of keeping the car between the middle line and the edge of the road.

It is a wild ride down the Swiss mountains. He veers from one side of the road to the other, first onto the icy patches at the side of the road, causing the car to skid for a few yards then returns to the hard surface of the bitumen, but only for a few moments. The next minute we are straddling the middle line. Fortunately, so far, no one is coming in the opposite direction. He is driving way too fast. I am beside myself in the back seat and Sandie, who is sitting next to Mike, is by this time nearly hysterical. When we round a hairpin bend, all control is lost. The car skids off the road into a boulder, which is the only thing stopping us from flying off the side of the mountain.

Luckily, we are only badly shaken and not hurt, but my knees are trembling so badly that they can hardly bear my weight when I try to step out of the car. I take a tentative step forward, hit an ice patch and end up on my bottom, only just stopping short of sliding down the mountain.

A siren sounds in the distance. It's the police. When they arrive at the scene, they demand that we pay a hundred dollars for the damage we have done to the rock. Surely they are joking. This must be some kind of weird Swiss humour. But their faces are deadly serious.

Mike refuses to pay up, gets into the car and prepares to drive on. We beg him to pay. It makes me nervous when the police have guns in their holsters. I hold my breath. The police tell us that if we don't pay we will be detained at the border and put into jail until we do.

Sandie and I scratch around in our purses to see what we can come up with. Finally

Mike reaches into his pocket for his wallet, something he hasn't done too often during this trip. We almost expect moths to fly out.

Mum and Dad would have a fit if they knew I was in the car with this lunatic—especially Mum. She would not allow me out the front door before she gave my dates a long, embarrassing lectures about driving carefully and how she did not want me disfigured for life in a car accident. Probably she was worried I wouldn't get married and she'd be stuck with me forever.

Oh so very frustrating!

I lie face down, my arms are bent, my palms flat. I am trying hard to lift my body off the ground. Dad's offered me ten pounds if I can do ten male push-ups. I've been trying all week without success. Today I've been at it for an hour and am in a lather of sweat. I can lift the top part of my body, but it's as if the lower part's glued to the ground. Dad's laughing at me. "You can do it, Sucat," he says. But I can't. My brother lies down next to me and does ten push-ups no probs! Grrrrh!

Chapter 22

CINQUECENTO

It is love at first sight!

When we arrive at the car yard in Amsterdam, Holland, it catches my eye straight away. It is bright yellow, my favourite colour, and gleams in the morning sun. We are here to buy a car, as all the tennis guys have told us this is the best place to do it.

A car, Sandie and I have decided, is essential. The trip with Mike was the last straw! Apart from that we are both sick to death of trying to cadge lifts with the other players, many of whom have also turned out to be the most atrocious drivers. Catching trains and having to lug all our bags, rackets and numerous silver cups up and down the railway platforms is too much like hard work. And as for hitchhiking, we've had too many bad experiences.

It says on the back it is a Fiat 500–Cinquecento. When I move closer and peer inside, I can see that the upholstery is black and the back two seats fold down, which is ideal. We'll have plenty of boot space for the heaps of junk we cart around with us. We make up our minds that although it is small, it is big enough for the two of us. Judging from the smile on the salesman's face, it's the quickest sale he's ever made. We bundle all our stuff into the back, then climb in and drive away with smiles so wide, we feel like our faces are going to crack!

Anyone for tea?

It's afternoon tea time. I can hear the rattle of tea cups in the sunroom. Tea is always important but today Mum has her best cloth on the table and the beautiful fine china cups and saucers from her glory box. She only uses them for special occasions. Aunty Nena's visiting. I'm so glad because I've been waiting for ages to ask her some questions. Aunty Nena is always more forthcoming than Mum, who never wants to tell me anything. I want to know, "How will I know when I meet Mister Right? And how does it work, that everyone gets one?" I'd hate to miss out. It's bad enough if I get selected last at tunnel ball. They both smile at me. Then Aunty Nena says, "You'll just know!"

Chapter 23

VIGO

When I wake up in the morning, I can hear the sound of waves crashing gently onto sand and smell salt in the air. I am totally disorientated. It is a familiar feeling, no doubt the result of moving to a different place every week. Memories of the beach at Narrabeen float into my mind. I feel my heart swell. When I look around the room I see the usual mess of plastic bags full of sweaty, dust-covered tennis clothes. My well-worn sandshoes are strewn across the floor, last night's magenta dress is draped over a chair and several Dunlop Maxply rackets are leaning on the wall near the door. Still half asleep, I wander over to the glass door leading to the balcony and slide it back. I am greeted by gusts of salty air. Then I remember! I am in Vigo, in the provence of Gallicia on the north-western coast of Spain, staying in a hotel right on the beach. I am in heaven. It seems like an eternity since I have been near the beach.

After breakfast, we head for the tennis club, which certainly leaves the tin sheds in Australia for dead. The club house of the Club de Campo de Vigo is one huge, open room with high ceilings, lots of windows and gleaming polished floors, and is surrounded by palms and lush tropical gardens. The sun is pouring in. The draw for the week is already posted on the notice board and when I cast my eye over it, I see that once again there are not many women playing in the tournament. The bad news is that unless one of us has an accident, it looks like Sandie and I will meet in the final. I am not looking forward to this, because up until now we have been taking it in turns to win.

The consolation is that I am in love. His name is Pascuale Riccardo. He is Italian and drop dead gorgeous with dark cornflower blue eyes, black wavy hair, light olive skin *and* he can sing. He is in fact the lead singer with the band that plays at the tennis club. Each night I sit enraptured as he sings love songs to me in French, Italian and Spanish in his husky voice. The only slight glitch is that he is a couple of inches shorter than me, but I remedy this by walking around with my knees bent, just in case I run into him.

At the end of the week Sandie and I end up playing against each other in the finals. It is a torrid match and although I win, it is not a happy experience. We both find it hard playing against each other because we are such good friends. By the end of the match, the conflict of emotions has got us to the point that we are not speaking. We only flop our hands at each other at the net.

Over breakfast the following morning, Sandie and I decide that we are going to give up smoking. We don't smoke all that much unless we are at a party. But all the free cigarettes we scored at the tournaments in England, which were mostly sponsored by cigarette companies, are now gone. American cigarettes are very expensive in Spain and the alternative, Spanish cigarettes—especially the ones with black tobacco—although cheaper, unfortunately smell quite obnoxious and seem to give the local population permanent bronchitis.

I have had to say my fond farewells to Pascuale the night before. He didn't finish work until 4.30am and wasn't going to be up when we left. But he will be playing in a club in Madrid in a couple of weeks' time, he tells me, so we organise to catch up then.

When we hop in the car Sandie and I are still uptight after the previous day's match, so it probably isn't the best of ideas to try to quit smoking at this particular time. After only a couple of hours on the road, when boredom and nicotine deprivation start to set in, we decide to throw the towel in. We pull over for a *café con leche* and buy a packet of Winston super largos. A few puffs and a couple of slurps later and the situation between us eases. We are back on an even keel—best of friends again! Just as well. Being stuck in such a confined space in our Cinquecento for the trip from Vigo to Barcelona (over 900 kilometres) and not talking would be an unbearable situation.

Cheats never prosper—or do they?

*I'm so excited! I'm playing in my first tournament, the under thirteen championships at White City—**the** venue for tennis in NSW. It's the first time I've played on grass. I'm in the semi-finals. Every time I hit a ball near the line the umpire calls it out. Every time my opponent hits a ball near the line it is in. I don't know what to do. Mum doesn't say anything. She just sits on the sideline knitting. After the match we find out that the umpire is the mother of the girl I played against.*

Chapter 24

ME ENCANTA BARCELONA

When we finally arrive in Barcelona, slightly the worst for wear, we are delighted to find that there are lots of Australian players at the tournament, including Ken Rosewall and my brother John. Although Sandie gets homesick, I never do. I love everything about Spain—the food, the language, the men, and here in Barcelona, the wonderful buildings—particularly the Gaudi ones—the wide Avenidas, especially Las Ramblas—wandering down it in the early evenings before dinner is heaven. Sometimes, instead of eating dinner we just eat tapas.

When I check the draw, once again I see that I am in for an easy time. My first decent match will be when I play Ana Maria Estelella in the semis. I haven't lost to her yet so unless disaster strikes, I will end up making the finals in both the singles and the doubles. This is excellent news, because the Barcelona Open is one of the first tournaments with decent prize money. Although our status as players has changed recently from registered players to professionals, it hasn't meant much when it comes to the bottom line at most of the tournaments we have played in so far, especially for women.

Although Billie Jean King has been beating the drum in the US very loudly and successfully, the European and English tournaments are way behind in paying women players. In fact it's not until 1973 that the US Open becomes the first major to offer equal pay, after Billie threatened to organise a boycott of the tournament.

Fortunately, Sandie is on the other side of the draw this week so we won't have any more dramas between us. She will have to beat Helga Schultz, who is number one in Germany and number eight in the world, to make the finals.

Towards the end of the week, my brother John and I lose in the semi-finals of the mixed to the Mandarinos. I am really pissed off. In my opinion, we could have won easily if John didn't insist on being so gentlemanly and serving second serves to Carmen. Senor Mandarino certainly doesn't repay the courtesy, pelting down his first serves as hard as he can to me, as well as hitting any stray balls, especially smashes, right at me.

We watch Ken Rosewall play a match against the Spanish champion, Manuel Arantes, which he loses due to "hometown umpiring". Every close ball is called in Arantes' favour. Poor Ken tries to keep the balls well in the court to avoid having them called out—without success. Ken is such an amazing man; ever graceful in this undeserved defeat, his behaviour and superb sportsmanship are exemplary and he doesn't even let his annoyance show. Not like me—I am furious just watching.

Helga Schultz wins against Sandie in the semi-finals, so I have to play her in the final. I don't like my chances against Helga and I am right. She is just too good, powering me off the court from both sides. It doesn't help that I have mostly been majoring in the minor tournaments, with a definite preference for location over the more prestigious events with better players. I am rarely stretched. I am certainly not used to Helga's fast and furious pace, especially on the backhand side. She really thumps the ball!

The doubles final also turns out to be a nightmare. Helga is playing with her sister Margaret, who has been trying to sell us expensive tennis pants in the ladies change room. Without success, I might add! I have other plans for my money. The boutiques on Calle de Serrano are calling to me loudly. All through the match, both of them just aim and fire every ball straight at our bodies when we are at the net. I am hit so many times I feel like a punching bag.

I am a bit of a prima donna at the best of times, but by the end of the match, I am seething. I leave the court and head for the refuge of the ladies' change room, just managing to lock myself in the loo, before the tears spill out. Sandie, always a much better sport than me, stays and dutifully shakes hands. But who cares! When I count my earnings for the week, I find that I have won $5,000, the most I've won at any tournament. In fact, it is more than the sum of my total career earnings to date. It's a fortune!

I'm in love

I go for a walk on the beach with my tennis coach. There's no one else around. He takes my hand and squeezes it. Shivers go up my arm. He touches my shoulder. Electric shocks race all around my body. He pulls me towards him. His body is hard. I can feel every part of him. He kisses me. My whole body trembles. I desperately want something to happen but don't know what it is. I turn my face towards him and smile. I'm only 11 but I'm in love.

Chapter 25

MADRID

On the way back up the highway to Madrid, I can feel the $5,000 I've won at the Barcelona Open burning a hole in my pocket. This is more money than I have ever dreamed of having at one time and I can hardly wait to start spending it!

Sandie and I barely spend a waking moment in the gorgeous hotel we are staying at. Nor do we pick a racket up all week. In fact, we don't even think of picking one up. We have a ball just doing ordinary things for a change. Instead of spending hours racing sweat-soaked around the court playing torrid matches, we wander down my favourite street, Calle de Serrano, checking out all the wonderful clothes in the boutiques housed in ornate art deco buildings, or head downtown to Gallerias Preciados and Cortes Ingles, the Spanish equivalents of David Jones and Myer. Time flies.

On the way we sip I don't know how many delicious *café con leches* in glamorous sidewalk cafes full of fascinating, beautifully dressed, impeccably groomed Madrilenos who I find hard not to stare at. I even go back to the Café Gijon to see if I can catch another look at that gorgeous bloke. No luck.

Oh well, I decide. Time to move on. He is only a dream and as the senora had told me when I'd discussed the matter with her, good-looking men can be nothing but trouble.

And anyway Pascuale is in Madrid now and even though he is a bit on the short side, he is a good-looking sort *and* he can sing!

Each night we either eat a delicious meal in one of our favourite restaurants or go around the dimly lit tapas bars off the Puerta del Sol where we drink robust red wine for two pesetas a glass, which includes a tapa. Some nights, Pascuale, who is playing at the Lagasca nightclub, comes out to dinner with us. But he is a spoilsport. He gets really annoyed about us eating so much garlic. He reckons we stink of it. And we probably do. But we are both totally addicted. We can't resist having garlic chicken every night and always eat up, much to Pascuale's distain, all the cloves of garlic on the side of the plate. Sometimes there are ten.

After dinner we go to the club where Pascuale is working. I find it so romantic when he sings to me. And certainly a step-up being courted this way. Although it appears Pascuale isn't into rushing things. He hasn't even tried to kiss me yet. I'm not sure whether it's because of my garlic consumption, our height difference or that he is just old-fashioned. Sandie and I usually don't make it back to our hotel until after four in the morning and the night porter at the hotel looks at us wide-eyed, not knowing what to make of us at all.

I feel like I belong in Madrid and wish I could stay forever, but sadly we have to leave because we are due to play in a tournament in Yugoslavia. After dinner on our last night, we check the map over and more or less think we know where we are going. It is 1,560 kilometres from Madrid to Opatija. It's going to be a *long* trip.

Pascuale arrives just as we are packing the car ready to leave. "I've come to teach you how to double shuffle," he tells us. The night before, when Sandie and I had told him about the ongoing trouble we've been having with grinding the gears in our little Fiat, Pascuale was unable to contain himself. He burst into an uncontrollable fit of laughter. It turns out that the bloody mechanics we've been taking the car to all over Madrid, to fix the grating sound that happens every time we change gears, have been ripping us off.

"The Fiat 500 has no synchromesh between gears," Pascuale manages to squeak out between giggles.

That doesn't mean much to us.

According to Pascuale, we are supposed to double shuffle the gears each time we change them. This turns out to be no mean feat and involves taking the gear back to neutral, letting the clutch out, then pushing it back in and putting it into gear in one fell swoop. Although we do quite a bit of practice, neither of us is quite able to get the hang of it before we leave or rather the timing. A lot of grating, grinding and kangarooing goes on. It doesn't help that quite a crowd amasses in front of the hotel to watch the goings on. Funny, they didn't tell us about "no synchromesh" when we bought the car, but I suppose Sandie and I were both short on Dutch and so excited about buying the car, we probably didn't get the finer points. And anyway, even if they had said something, we wouldn't have cared less. We've been grinding the gears ever since and have had to replace the clutch plate twice.

We can't delay any longer so we squeeze the rest of our stuff into the back of the car, only just managing to get the boot closed. Our little Fiat is packed to the rafters. By this time all the hotel staff, who have watched our comings and goings all week with such amusement, have come out to watch. When we finally squish ourselves into the front, we end up with our noses practically on the dashboard and are barely able to see out of the rear-vision as we kangaroo our way onto the main road.

I am sad to be leaving Madrid, again. We've had such a fantastic time. And I will miss Pascuale desperately, especially his cornflower blue eyes with those long lashes. They truly are to die for.

At the breakfast table

Dad's reading the paper. Mum's making toast. I smile to myself. I have a very special secret. Mum and Dad would kill me if they found out. My tennis coach is sitting at the other end of the table eating his breakfast. I steal a glance at him. My face feels hot. My body tingles. I close my eyes and remember what it feels like when he touches me. I don't look at him again. If I do, I'll give the game away.

Chapter 26

YUGOSLAVIA

We totally underestimate how long the trip will take and end up having to drive right through the better part of two nights to make it on time for our first tournament in Opatija. We arrive absolutely buggered! When I glance into the rear-vision mirror before getting out of the car, it is not a good look. My eyes are red and bloodshot, my hair and skin are greasy. When I look down, my clothes are food-stained and crumpled. I take a deep breath and nearly keel over. My head is dizzy from lack of sleep. When I try to get out of the car my legs are *so* stiff from being stuck in such a small space for so long, it feels like rigor mortis has set in.

At that very moment, the tournament director rushes up, yelling at us that we are very late and are due to go straight onto the court to play or we'll be forfeited. I move towards the change room as fast as I can under the circumstances, and then stagger towards the court. My racket, which I haven't picked up during our week in Madrid, nor during these last couple of days in the car, feels heavy—always a bad sign. Not surprisingly, Sandie and I both lose our matches decisively.

But there are compensations. We are staying in an extremely elegant old hotel and Opatija is a charming town full of lovely old buildings with white domed roofs huddled along cobbled streets, perched on the edge of the Adriatic Sea.

One thing I'm glad about is that Boris, my Yugoslavian boyfriend who organised for Sandie and me to play in these tournaments, was sent at the last minute with a team to Germany. It could have been awkward otherwise. I've gone right off him since I've met Pascuale.

Our next tournament is in Belgrade and although the road we head out of town on is a main highway, it is in very poor condition. It is so full of potholes and odd sections of unsealed road that we have to drive slowly and carefully. A breakdown would be a disaster. There are very few other cars on the road, and definitely no NRMA to call for roadside assistance. The only service station we see all day is back in Opatija.

Although the trip is just under 500 kilometres, because of the condition of the road, we average only about 45 kilometres an hour. As Sandie and I never manage to get an early start, we aren't able to make it in one day. In the late afternoon, we start looking for somewhere to stay for the night and begin to get a bit worried when it starts to get dark. There aren't any hotels along the road like there have been in all the other countries we've been in. Finally, we stop and ask some English people who are having a cup of tea by the side of the road.

"For some reason," they tell us, "under the communist system, each town is allocated a certain number of hotels depending on its size. You'll have to turn off to one of the towns."

We take the next turnoff to God knows where! Half the letters are upside down but there is a five after the writing. We hope that means it's only five miles or kilometres away. We finally arrive at a small village, after driving down a road that is in even worse condition than the highway where we find a hotel. At the reception counter, a small plump lady advises us that the hotel, the only one in the town, is full. However, she smiles and beckons us to follow her. We aren't sure what to make of the situation but we are so tired by this time, we are prepared to give anything a go. We traipse after her, up and down stairs, down narrow cobbled lanes until finally we end up in what appears to be the home of either a friend or a relative, who we gather rents out rooms.

We are also starving and make hand signals about where we can get something to eat. The two ladies talk with each other again. Then the second one signs us to follow her. She leads us up and down more stairs, through more buildings and down other narrow, cobbled lanes to someone else's lounge room which is all set up with tables and chairs. The good news is that people are eating.

Sandie insists she wants chicken. I tell her to forget it because the only words we know in Yugoslavian at this stage are *desno, levo* and *ravno* (right, left and straight ahead), which I can't see being much help at all in this particular situation. All our other communications so far have been by actions. But when the waiter comes around, I nearly die of embarrassment when Sandie starts making chook noises and flapping her elbows. The other diners turn around and stare. I try to shrink under the table but find it difficult because at the same time I am trying to control a fit of giggles. I'm certainly glad we don't know anyone. In the end, however, despite all these excellent efforts, we are served pork with rice enveloped in pickled cabbage leaves. When I look around I see everyone else is eating the same thing.

When we finally arrive in Belgrade, we find that once again the organisers have not stinted on our accommodation.

The Balkan Hotel is gorgeous, as are the Yugoslavian men, we decide. In the early evening, we sit on the balcony at the front of the hotel sipping strong Turkish coffee, and check them out. It seems they are all tall, dark and handsome with the most amazing high cheekbones. They are also dressed beautifully in Italian clothes. We decide to redo our "top sort" ranking system for the men tennis players and place the Yugoslavs at number one, this position having previously been held by the Spanish. That pushes the English, who were only hanging by a thread due to that gorgeous specimen of manhood, Roger Taylor, out of the top ten.

Top Ten Rankings:
Yugoslavians
Spanish
Italians
Mauritians (although I've only met one)
Jamaicans (although I've only met two)
Argentinians
Chileans
Australians
Americans
South Africans

Sandie and I each receive several marriage proposals during the week. Although Yugoslavia appears to be quite liberal under the dictator Tito, in reality it isn't. People can't just leave the country if they want to. Apparently marrying a foreign woman is the best way to get out.

It is not our finest hour of tennis at the Belgrade tournament. We both lose early on in both the singles and the doubles. We are the only non-communists in the event. It is a very strong field of hefty Eastern European women. The weather is damp, and the courts are so slow that you can almost chase a passing shot. Our extra-curricular activities are excessive. We are out and about in town with Bojan and Aleksandar, two uni students we met at the hotel, every night.

Oooh what a feeling!

Julia's mum is not at home. My tennis coach and I are upstairs in the bedroom. Kissing. He puts his hand down the front of my shirt. It feels incredible. Like small, tickly trembles. He moves his hand onto my nipple. My whole body goes wild! I hear someone creaking up the stairs. The door opens. "I know what you're up to," Julia says. I blush from head to toe, jump off the bed, race downstairs and out the front door. I hope she won't tell anyone my secret. If she does there will be big trouble

Chapter 27

ROMANIA

We can feel that Romania is a lot different to Yugoslavia as soon as we cross the border at Timisoara. Gypsies in horse-drawn carts are driving up and down the road. The countryside has a grim, uncared-for look about it. The few other cars on the road, which we pass, are large American rust-bucket relics from the Second World War. The road is even worse. The people we encounter look sad and do not return our smiles. It also drizzles steadily most of the way, which doesn't help matters. When we finally arrive, we find our hotel is very dreary, damp and dark. We feel depressed and try to ring some friends in England but the line is so bad we can't get through.

We decide against dining at the hotel and drive into the centre of Bucharest where we find that there are only three restaurants, which are all very expensive. But we *have* to eat! When we finish our meal and the waiter plunks the bill down on our table, we discover much to our discomfort that dinner costs even more than we've calculated. We find ourselves in the embarrassing situation of not having enough Romanian money to pay, not wanting to change too much money at the border. Drachmas can't be changed back, nor can they be used anywhere else. As we are also being paid in drachmas for playing in the tournament we would end up being stuck with those we don't spend—a terrible state of affairs.

The restaurant manager sends one of the waiters with us to a nearby hotel to change our money. On the way, people keep coming up to us, trying to get us to change our American dollars with them—offering us incredibly high rates, almost twice as much as what we got at the border. Although we are tempted, we don't dare, especially after the waiter tells us in his broken English that we could go to jail if we get caught. Our hotel is bad enough. I can't imagine what the jails would be like.

Fortunately, the next morning things start to look up. A tournament official comes to tell us that we stayed at the wrong hotel last night. All the players from the other communist countries are staying at our current hotel, but we are to be installed in a different one. They move us straight away. Once we've settled in at our new and much more upmarket hotel, we discover we've been assigned a spy. Vlad, a small, nuggetty man keeps following us around, even sitting with us when we eat. He also tries to persuade us to catch the bus with him to the tennis club but we jump in the car and take off, leaving him in front of the hotel shaking his head and madly waving his hands at us.

We arrive at the Belgrade tennis club looking pretty scrubby in our jeans and tops, still wrinkled from the trip, having been unable to get the iron in our room to work. But compared to the locals, we look like a couple of film stars. Their clothes look like discards from second-hand shops except, that is, for Tiriac and Nastaste, Romania's top two players, who pull up shortly after us in a shiny, new Ford Mustang. Both of them are wearing the most beautiful suede suits. Obviously they operate under different rules than the masses.

Halfway through the week Vlad gets the flick. Sandie and I feel a bit guilty about it because he's told us how much he enjoys the job, in particular because he gets to eat better food at our table. Admittedly we have been most uncooperative, avoiding him totally whenever possible. But in retrospect, we certainly wouldn't have exhibited such bravado if we'd known about Nicolae Ceausescu, the current dictator, known for his brutality, repression and hard-line measures, killing off anyone who didn't agree with his policies.

Once again we are the only players from non-communist countries competing in the tournament. While Sandie and I sit in front of the club house sipping big black, very strong, sweet Turkish coffees and smoking, the other women, who are all built like Amazons, spend their spare time pounding around the oval adjoining the tennis club or hitting up. We lose in the early rounds of the singles but manage to make it to the semis of the doubles losing to two Czech amazons in drizzling rain, which plays havoc with our gut strung rackets. I play most of the match with one of my racket strings broken.

Early one morning, as we walk around the city centre, elderly women dressed in long black dresses are sweeping the street. The people we pass keep their eyes downcast. No matter *how hard* we try, we just can't get them to crack a smile. We are going shopping to try to spend the 50 drachmas we've received for playing in the tournament. We've been trying to spend them all week, unsuccessfully, by having facials and our nails done, but those services only cost half a drachma. Today, as a last resort, we are going to a large department store but when we arrive we find there is nothing to buy there either. The dresses are all the same and look like uniforms—in one style and one colour, red. There is nothing that we are interested in. The little stock that is on display looks like it has come out of Noah's ark!

All the women look enviously at our jeans as we walk around town and we receive several approaches to buy them. In the end we find some red fabric with gold embroidery, which I think is rather garish but Sandie says will make nice curtains or a bedspread. But who would want curtains or a bedspread?

"Things must really be desperate in Romania," Sandie says when we get back to the hotel and discover that someone has stolen my well-worn Bonds Cottontails off the little clothesline on our balcony.

The trip back to Spain is a nightmare. Somehow we completely lose our way and end up way off course and on the road to Paris. It isn't really so very surprising because we don't have a proper map. What's amazing is that we've managed thus far. We try to circumnavigate Paris by taking the *Periferique*, the ring road, but end up in the middle of the city instead. Of course, we don't have a road map of Paris either so we drive around and around in endless circles, always finishing up back at the Seine, having gone back and forth over I don't know how many bridges. It takes us hours to find our way out. It is in fact a miracle that we ever do. It is well after 11pm by the time we finally drive through the outskirts of the city.

We've missed both lunch and dinner and are starving. But unfortunately everything is closed in the small village we pull into. The only place we eventually find where we can get something to eat that is still open is a bar. The drinkers in the front section, who are by this time ruddy faced and well underway, give us a rousing reception as we come in the front door. Luckily, the bar owner ushers us into the back room which is almost filled by a great big oak table and long benches. He informs us that the only thing he can offer us is bread and cheese and a glass of wine. It sounds terrific. I am so hungry that I would even have considered eating horse, which is considered a local delicacy, by this stage! A few moments later he comes back with a round of brie and a camembert the size of large dinner plates, a huge loaf of fresh bread and a bottle of wine. Not used to the hearty appetites of women tennis players, he is absolutely astounded when we polish off the lot in no time at all. Although I have to admit that afterwards, as I make my way out of the bar, I feel decidedly queasy. And have never felt quite the same about brie or camembert again!

By the time we get back into the car, it is one in the morning. We drive down the street of the small village, stopping at various places to see if we can stay there but can't rouse anyone, except for one bloke who yells at us from his upstairs window. I am quite sure that he is telling us to piss off in French. The wine is making us *so* sleepy that we have to take it in turns to drive, but only manage about ten minutes each. In the end we pull over and sleep in the car at the side of the road.

We spend the most *dreadful* night. Crammed into the front of our Fiat 500, our noses once again almost on the dashboard, freezing cold with an icy wind whipping around the car, it is unbearable. When we wake in the morning, the windscreen wipers are iced into place. We are both as stiff as boards and have trouble starting the car.

It's not all right!

He slides his hand down the front of my dress. My small breasts ache to be touched. He explores my body with his fingers. Every part of me goes wild. He slides his hand underneath the elastic of my pants. His fingers gently push inside me. My body feels like it's about to explode! "It'll be all right," he whispers. He undoes his zipper, eases his pants down and pulls out his penis. It's sticks straight out. "It's all right. You won't get pregnant," he says. "You haven't had your periods yet." I'm horrified. I break free and run away as fast as I can.

Chapter 28

ME ENCUENTRO MUY SOLA

No sooner have we arrived back in Spain from Yugoslavia than Sandie tells me she is missing her family dreadfully. She decides she wants to go back home to Australia straight away. I try to persuade her to stay, without success. Within a week she has booked her ticket and has her bags packed ready to go.

I watch her plane race down the runway and take off into a clear, blue Castilian sky, then walk back through the airport to my car, taking deep breaths in order to hold back my tears. I just manage to make it to the car, jump in and slam the door before they tumble down my face. I don't want anyone to see me cry, so I sit in the car until I finally collect myself. It is late afternoon when I finally drive back to our rooms in General Oraa. Although I feel alone and scared, I am not ready to go back to Australia.

Now that Sandie has gone home, things aren't the same between Pascuale and me. Perhaps it is the fact that it has always been the three of us who went everywhere together. But I believe that Pascuale too has changed, now that Sandy isn't here. He wants me to stay at home with the wives of the other band members who are all married with children, instead of going to the Clubs to watch him sing at night. Also, now there's just the two of us, we don't seem to have anything to talk about. Not like when there were three. We were never at a loss for words. Now we just sit there. It is only when he sings to me in his husky voice, looking at me with those cornflower blue eyes, that things are anywhere near the same. Then he starts to nag me about smoking. He says it ruins his voice—which it probably does! But when he tells me "no garlic" it is the last straw. Life without garlic would be impossible. There are just some things which aren't negotiable.

Now I've done it! I am all by myself without Sandie or Pascuale. I feel very lonely, especially at the end of the day. All the tournaments have finished for the year and I am now coaching. During the seemingly endless hours after work, I have *nothing* to do except to wait until it's time to go for dinner. Restaurants in Madrid don't open until 9.30pm. It is autumn and the evenings are way too dark and cold to walk up and down the street. Not that I feel like doing any more exercise, after a full day of giving tennis lessons. I am stuck here in my windowless room without anyone to talk to, or any books to read. I've already given the once over to this month's *Women's Own*, which I find the most boring magazine on earth. Senora Dona Ana always invites me in to watch the television with her but I generally stay in my room because I find not being able to understand what they say is too frustrating for words. My Spanish at this stage isn't good enough. I even have trouble understanding the ads.

So it's a case of sitting and watching the hands of the clock until it is 9 o'clock and at last time to get ready to go for dinner at the little restaurant down the road. There at least I can console myself with good food and wine. The same solitary diners greet me each evening, only momentarily glancing up from their plates or reading their evening papers. I always have the same thing—*menestra de verduras* (mixed vegetables) followed by *pollo al ajillo,* (garlic chicken) washed down with a half bottle of Rioja. The wine makes me feel light-headed and once home I fall on the bed and escape into the oblivion of sleep. *Why* do I stay? Why don't I just pack my bags and go home too?

The following morning, I write a list of the reasons why I don't want to go home:

1. I don't want to run into my old tennis coach.
2. Dad will tell me what to do and try and marry me off to an accountant.
3. I will end up locked away in a dreary, windowless, cell-like room tap-tap-tapping my life away, working as some boring person's secretary.
4. Harry will certainly have married that schoolteacher by now.
5. I can't be me, whoever that is?
6. I like being incognito, living a secret life, and enjoy the fact that nobody knows exactly where I am.
7. I really do love Spain. Here I am Senorita Susana—a completely different person from that Susan who lives in Narrabeen.

I'm just having trouble adjusting to life by myself again.

I'm broken-hearted

My tennis coach has gone to play tennis in a tournament in Tasmania. I miss him so much I can hardly bear it. When I collect the mail from the box today, there's a letter from him. I'm so excited—I can't wait to see what he says.

"Dear Sue, When I come back to Sydney, I won't be coming to coach you. I think it's better if we don't see each other anymore."

What does he mean? I don't understand. Why doesn't he want to see me anymore?

Chapter 29

ME SIGO ENCONTRANDO MUY SOLA

I run into Charlie Payne outside the apartment block where I am living. He is an American I've met a couple of times around the neighbourhood. He asks me if I'd like to go out for a meal. I am not that keen, because he comes over as a bit of a sleaze bag. But I feel dreadfully lonely. It is Christmas and I am a long way from home. There haven't been any pre-Chrissie drinks and parties in Madrid. Christmas here is a solemn, religious occasion. All the Spanish people I know have gone to ground. Nothing much is open and there are hardly any cars on the streets. I haven't even received any letters from home. So I agree to go.

When I tell Senora del Puerto, the garrulous one of the two senoras who I am now living with (much to the chagrin of the other senora, but I couldn't face winter in that cold, windowless bedroom), that I am going out with Charlie, she isn't impressed. She has no time for him at all. He is, in her opinion, *"una sinverguenza"* a worthless good-for-nothing. He has a bad reputation in the neighbourhood for not paying his bills, she tells me. If you ask me, you should tell him to *"vaya y hacer gargaros por alli"*, she says, flinging her arms around. It's one of the senora's favourite expressions, which I'm sure means piss off.

We go to the Restaurant Magerit in the Eurobuilding, an American hotel in Chamartin, where we have a nice if dull lunch both food and conversation-wise. My suspicions are confirmed that Charlie is definitely on the slippery side. I can't quite put my finger on exactly what it is about him. He is certainly evasive about everything, even where he lives and what he does for a living. I only just manage to squeeze out of him after considerable effort and several glasses of red that he lives here in the Eurobuilding and is a racing car driver. But I don't believe him. He looks way too old to race cars. He must be at least 50. His ruddy complexion also intimates that he hits the grog. What nails it for me is when the bill arrives. After a flurry of pocket searching, he tells me that he has forgotten to bring his wallet with him. He asks me to pay, promising faithfully to fix me up as soon as the banks re-open after the holiday period.

When I get home, the senora gives me heaps. "I told you about that bloody *sin verguenza*," she says, wringing her hands in despair and following up with, "Just wait until I see him in the street, he'll be sorry."

Early in the New Year, when my car starts to overheat I ring Charlie. Although he still hasn't paid me back, I am desperate. He is the only person I am acquainted with who knows anything about cars. He also told me over lunch at Christmas that he has an excellent mechanic who is honest and reasonably priced, not something I've previously encountered in Spain. He instructs me to bring the car over to his place and he'll take it to the garage for me.

Four days go by and I still haven't heard a word from Charlie about the car. When I ring and ask him what is going on, he tells me that it is quite a serious problem, and that the mechanic is waiting for some parts to come in. It will be ready in a couple of days, he assures me. I am not happy. Charlie's story sounds a bit fishy to me so I decide to catch a cab around to his place to see what is really going on. Just as I arrive, I see Charlie driving off in *my* car!

"Follow that car," I screech at the taxi driver, pointing at my little yellow Fiat as it disappears around the corner.

I duck my head down low as we head out of town in hot pursuit. About fifteen kilometres out of town, way out in the middle of nowhere, Charlie turns off the main road into a large warehouse complex. I pay the taxi driver, who looks like he's enjoyed every minute of the exercise, jump out and race over to Charlie.

"So what's going on with the car? I need it now," I tell him.

"You can't take it now," he says. "It might blow up as you're driving along."

"I don't care," I reply. "I can't do without it. I'll have to take the risk."

I can see that I've got Charlie by the short and curlies. He can't do anything but agree. He asks me for a lift back to town, saying that he'll be able to help me if anything happens on the way. What can I do but agree, albeit reluctantly? When I hop into the driver's seat and glance at the petrol gauge I notice it is on empty. The tank had been full when I'd left the car with Charlie. The snake must have been driving up a storm all over Madrid, because my little car goes forever on a tank of petrol.

"There's a garage just a couple of ks down the road," Charlie says, "where we can stop and fill up."

Charlie insists on doing the honours at the pump, then grabs the hundred peseta note out of my hand and races over to pay at the office.

Back in town, after I drop him off, when I take a look at the gauge, it is on empty again. I can't believe it. The bloody deviate! He's got me for my hundred pesetas, I don't have any petrol, and I still haven't got my money back for his share of the lunch. I burst into a fit of giggles. I decide not to mention this little scenario to the senora. She'll really think I am a duffer if she hears about this little effort! And she won't be far wrong.

I'm so miserable

My body aches all over. I can't sleep. Nights go on forever. I can't believe it. I keep asking myself, why? My mind won't stop still. Under the covers, I clench my fists. I will time to go backwards so that when I wake up in the morning, my tennis coach will be here to hit with me. But when I wake up, he isn't. And I know he won't be coming back. I bury all that has happened deep inside me. Then I rebel totally. I smoke, eat erratically and put on weight, party, sprout pimples, attack my hair with scissors and peroxide, don't go around with my "nice" friends anymore, misbehave at school, don't do my homework, can't concentrate, am grumpy, moody, generally obnoxious and hard to get on with.

Chapter 30

CARLOS

I decide to spend another winter in Madrid. I've been invited to coach at the Puerta de Hierro tennis club. It is *the* club in Madrid, according to Senora del Puerto who is very impressed by my new employment. I can see I have gone up in her estimation quite considerably. No doubt it will give her a certain level of kudos, as well as plenty to gossip about around the neighbourhood. All the members, she informs me, are from very g*ood* families. And the vast majority, I notice when I go to play there, have titles. However, it turns out that even in these higher echelons of society, there are not many women who come to play at the club. I am doing six or seven hours of lessons a day, generally with middle-aged men who are reasonably good players and just like to play sets with a good player. It is hard work, but I certainly prefer it to coaching beginners.

Carlos, who is a lot younger that the other members, tells me he is only a student and as much as he would like to, he can't afford to have tennis lessons with me. He speaks English very well. He informs me that his family lived in America for a couple of years when his father was transferred over there for work. I am always desperate to speak English so I really enjoy chatting with him. He asks me to go out with him the following Saturday.

On our first outing, Carlos and I catch the recently completed Teleferico, a cable car which runs from Paseo de Pintor Rosales to the Casa de Campo, the largest park in Madrid. From 40 metres up, we certainly get a bird's eye view over the city, the Manzanares river and the surrounding mountains. But I'm not into heights so I'm glad the journey is only ten minutes long. The Casa de Campo is a huge expanse of green with a lake, zoo, amusement park and café, which, Carlos tells me, was formerly a Royal hunting ground. We walk for miles because Carlos has very little money, and won't agree to me paying, or even going halves on any of the other diversions available.

When we get back to Madrid we walk up the Calle de Serrano and onto the Generalissimo, and then as he has a student pass for the Prado, we spend a few hours wandering around the gallery. My favourite paintings, I decide, are the Rubens and Titians, in particular those of generously proportioned, doe-eyed women frolicking or lazing around in woodland settings, who appear to almost be in a stupor and are seemingly oblivious to the fact that they are in the nude.

I also really admire Goya's paintings, especially in his dark days, and promise myself that I will come back again to examine these works more fully. My spirits always lift after spending time wandering around an art gallery, the Prado in particular. It has the additional benefit of having a lot of handsome Spanish art lovers to gaze at as well.

Carlos and I really get on well. He is a gentle kind of guy, an interesting conversationalist and certainly knows how to keep a girl entertained with minimum expenditure. When I tell the old senora about Carlos I can see I go up even higher in her estimation.

The bus wouldn't stop!

When I see the school special coming, I race around the back of the old house. When all the buses have gone, I walk to school—slowly. I don't want to go to school. I am miserable. At least this way I manage to miss Maths. I just know I'll never use algebra or geometry when I grow up. Anyway, I can't concentrate. "Susan could do better if she didn't spend all her time gazing out the window," according to my school report. I tell the teacher who catches me as I try to sneak into the classroom between periods, that the bus wouldn't stop. I hope the bus-driver doesn't get into trouble.

Chapter 31

REAL CLUB DE TENIS PUERTA DE HIERRO

The Puerta de Hierro tennis club is a beautiful place to work but the coaching side is another matter and not always an easy proposition. My pupils are very wealthy and used to getting their own way. One of the most difficult, the Marques de Santa Domingo, an extremely rich, multi- lingual Madrileno, walks around with his nose in the air. According to Senor Bonny, the manager at the club, he has never had to do a day's work in his life. Like the members of the Real Madrid Club, he lives off the income from his fincas (country estates) and investments. He spends his time travelling, studying and giving people, most of whom in his opinion are inferior, a hard time whenever he can—with relish.

For the past few weeks I've been coaching his wife, the Marquesa, and although she is by no means a sporty type, she listens very carefully to my instructions and has improved considerably. However, I don't like my chances with the Marques. I've already seen him with Alfonso (the other club coach) and observed that he doesn't take the least bit of notice of anything Alfonso says. He has no timing whatsoever and consistently sprays the balls all over the place. He starts off the same way with me. In order to counteract this, I suggest to him that he stand side-on with his racket back. When it is the right time for him to hit the ball, I will yell out "hit". By the look on his face I can see he is not happy with this proposal at all. He tells me he won't do it because he doesn't want to look like an idiot in front of the other club members who I notice have gathered at the back of the court to watch the proceedings.

From my point of view, he looks more of an idiot spraying the ball all over the place than he would ever do standing side-on with his racket back. But he waves his arms around and roars his refusal. There isn't much I can do for him so I spend the rest of the lesson feeding him balls he bangs the bejesus out of. At the end of the lesson he marches ahead of me off the court into the men's change room and in no time at all has showered, changed, and then with nose in the air, strode out of the club in a huff.

A few weeks later, I am challenged to a match by Alvaro, one of the young bucks from the illustrious Maranon family, who can't believe a man could possibly lose to a woman. Quite a few of the members place bets. When the word gets out that there is quite a large amount of money riding on the match, a large crowd gathers around the court. I feel a bit sorry for the bloke in a way because there is no way I am going to let him have a single point unless he earns it. It just isn't in my nature. Unfortunately for Alvaro, those points are few and far between. I put my nose down and really set my mind to the task at hand. My debonair opponent, kitted out in shiny, white garb, ends up in a lather of sweat with dirt stains down his once immaculate shirt. He puffs and pants, runs himself ragged, but doesn't get a game. In fact, hardly a point. It is extremely satisfying

My brother always says that I play a lot better when I play against men. It brings out my killer instinct. It must be as a result of all those death matches we played against each other as kids. Poor Alvaro was not to know.

One of the few women I coach is Maria Teresa. I feel sorry for the poor girl. She is always so downcast and miserable. Some days, when I give her a lesson, she just hangs her racket at her side like a wet dishrag, as though she doesn't have the energy to hold it up in front of her. Senor Bonny tells me that this is because her *novio* (boyfriend) of seven years has broken up with her, and subsequently none of the other men will have anything to do with her.

"Even though she probably didn't even kiss him, because Spanish girls are always chaperoned," he confides.

Seems a bit unfair and decidedly prehistoric to me, but apparently it is how things are in Spain during these Franco years. There is a palpable sense of the omnipresent Catholic Church, an ever-present God and an always-watching dictator monitoring every move and action people make—especially the women, it seems.

I am surprised when Carlos kisses me for the first time. I thought we were just good friends. Although we've been going out a couple of times a week for a few months, he hasn't even so much as tried to hold my hand. Not like those *phantom pouncers* back in Australia.

After that first kiss, he tells me that he loves me. I am even more surprised. Maybe I would be better off with someone like Carlos than the assortment of boyfriends I have encountered so far, I surmise. I know my parents would definitely approve of him—his good prospects, beautiful manners, neat conservative dress and intelligence. The fact that he always wears his hair nice and short would be a winner with Mum. Her requirements for her daughters' beaus are not so different from those of her more conservative Spanish sisters! Both of the senoras leave me in no doubts about where their sympathies lie.

Carlos is very nice and certainly excellent husband material, but I've always imagined being swept off my feet by a tall, dark and handsome man, like the one I saw at the Café Gijon.

Not really wagging it!

My new friend, Geraldine, and I decide not to attend the school swimming carnival. I'm a terrible swimmer—I don't like putting my face in the water and have to fight hard not to sink. "It's not really wagging it," she says. The Manly Wharf bus is approaching on the far side of the road. Geraldine takes off over Pittwater Road ahead of me. I follow in hot pursuit without looking either right or left. I end up on the top of the bonnet of a very surprised looking motorist, fortunately with only a large bruise from the Jaguar on the front of his car's bonnet. "You could have ended up under the tyres," says the driver, who is very shaken and offers to drive me home. We walk to the Collaroy Baths and the swimming carnival.

Chapter 32

UNA VISITA AL MONASTERIO CISTERCIENCE DE SANTA MARIA DE LA HUERTA, PROVINCIA DESORIA.

"We are an Order of Strict Observance here at Santa Maria de la Huerta," the priest tells Carlos and me, observing us with a definite air of disapproval—a young Spaniard and *"una extranjera"*, most probably indulging in sinful relations, his disdainful glance intimates. We wander past a large, very basic refectory where some priests are eating, then up a rough-hewn stone stairwell and down a series of long, dark stone corridors. Finally, when we pause in a small, bare room with slits for windows, he starts telling us his story. "We are a non-speaking order, but I have a dispensation to speak when I take tourists through the monastery. My name is Father John."

I am not a Catholic so it is difficult for me to understand this kind of thing. Who would agree to 'not speaking'? For me it would be like not breathing. Everyone I know would vouch for that! I decide to make the most of the fact that the priest is allowed to speak and press him for more details.

"What other strict observances do you have to adhere to?" I ask.

"We are only allowed to eat fruit and vegetables, which we grow in the gardens that you can see over there," he elaborates, waving his arm. "However, at the moment it is being discussed whether we will be getting a dispensation to eat eggs."

My mouth falls open, but he doesn't seem to notice. "As well as attending morning and evening masses, every day we must spend a minimum of seven hours on our knees praying."

Pretty tight schedule, I think. "And how did you come to be a priest in this order in the first place?" I can't resist asking.

"I am the second son in a large family. It is normal. The eldest takes on the family business and the second son goes into the priesthood to ensure the family's place in heaven. I am very fortunate because this is a very good order. There has always been enough to eat, and it was also one of the few safe havens for priests during the tumultuous period of the Civil War."

I decide I'm glad that I was born a girl in Australia *and not a Catholic*. After all, I am the second daughter and a convent might have seemed an attractive proposition to my father at several times during my teenage years! Later on, with a bit more encouragement, Father John tells me that each priest receives an allowance of a litre of virgin wine each day, which they also make on the premises.

After our tour, we eat at a restaurant nearby and try the virgin wine from the monastery. We only drink a couple of glasses each, but once back in the car we pass out for about three hours and wake up with the most dreadful pounding headaches. I feel like someone has hit me on the head with a brick, and my mouth tastes like it has been in drought for several years.

"Virgin wine is very high in alcohol, usually about 23% plus," Carlos explains.

No wonder those priests spend so long on their knees I think! The miracle is that they are able to get to their feet and walk around at all.

My first win

Although I'm still very much down in the dumps, I win my first tournament: the Canterbury Bankstown NSW Hardcourt Championship Under 12. The committee doesn't believe I'm eleven. They insist on seeing my birth certificate. I'm so much taller than the other girls, they say. I've grown six inches in the last six months and have put on weight. I look like a different person. I also feel like someone else. I'm a nothing and a no one. I don't know how to act or be. I try to copy Julia's personality.

Chapter 33

EL ABRIGO

I am so excited. I've just bought the most beautiful item of clothing I've ever owned. It is a Dr Zhivago-style coat, made from very fine bull's hide, coarse dark brown suede, with thick, lustrous woolly curls spilling out of the hood and cuffs, then wrapping around the hem. If I want to, I can also turn it inside out and wear just a mass of curls. Zhivago coats are all the rage now because of the movie *Dr Zhivago* with Omar Sharif, and this one is truly to die for!

I have never thought much about coats. The only one I've ever owned before was a pale blue wool car coat Mum made. But I just can't do without a coat here in Madrid, especially when it snows on the Sierra del Guadarrama. Icy winds rip right through me as they gust down the broad avenues. Some mornings when I arrive at the tennis club, the straw they cover the courts with overnight glistens with ice and crackles when I walk on it. One day it was minus two degrees and I played three sets in gloves, without even taking my track pants off. I definitely need a coat!

I buy it at Zorrillas, an establishment so posh I feel like shooting through when I arrive at the entrance. But Carlos is right there behind me so I can't. His mother, who I haven't met yet, has recommended it. My feet sink into the strip of plush red carpet as I make my way from the edge of the footpath to the front step, which is under an elaborate portico. Inside, it is even more intimidating! High, ornate ceilings, carpet which melts at my step, and worst of all, the very stylish, immaculately made-up/not-a-hair-out-of-place sales assistants. They totally intimidate me. Then there are the clients themselves!

I deeply regret not having dressed better for the occasion. As usual, I don't have any make-up on, my hair is pulled back in a rubber band (I am trying to grow it) and I am dressed in jeans, sweater and Ugg boots. I feel decidedly gauche and wish fervently that I could just slip away unnoticed. All eyes of the immaculately groomed, sylph-like creatures wafting around the interior of the shop follow my progress with their noses poised disdainfully in the air.

I press on courageously. Carlos is still right behind me, so what else can I do? To make matters worse, an elegant senora is trying on two different coloured mink coats in front of the mirror, unable to decide which one to take, the dark or the light. She ends up doing a Jackie Onassis and takes them both. By this stage, I am cringing with embarrassment but as I move to the lower level of the shop, my eyes lock onto a mass of dark, luxuriant curls hanging on a rack against the far wall. I am instantly and totally captivated!

After ignoring me for a considerable length of time, one of the haughty shop assistants finally asks if I would like to try it on. It is my size and despite my hair, lack of make-up and very ordinary attire, as soon as I put on this amazing coat, I undergo a dramatic transformation. I almost look like a fashion statement! Besides, I rationalise, when I nearly faint after looking at the price tag, it will come in handy, because Carlos and I are heading north for a few days.

The following morning, I can't resist donning my beautiful new coat when I go down to the local shop to pick up a few things for the trip and can hardly keep a straight face as I make my order because I don't have a stitch on underneath!

My first bra

*I'm dying to get my first bra. Everyone else in my class at school has one. Except me. Mum **finally** agrees I can have one. In Woolies I jig from one foot to another. The bras are in the last row. But Mum and Aunty Nena are taking forever going up and down the aisles. When we finally get there, Mum says she thinks I should get the sensible, cotton one. But I like the lacy one. "It'll itch you and will fall apart in the wash," Mum says. Then Aunty Nena looks at my chest. "I don't know what you think you're going to put into it," she says loudly. "If you ask me it's a waste of money." Everyone in Woolies turns to stare and make their own assessment of the situation. I run.*

Chapter 34

VAMOS AL NORTE

Mid-morning a few days later, Carlos and I get into my Fiat 500 and head north. After several hours on the road, we pull over to the side to eat our lunch of bocadillos. I have just swallowed the last piece of my sandwich when Carlos appears around my side of the car, opens the door and squeezes himself into the couple of inches of space beside me. He starts kissing me passionately. It is not a pleasurable experience, particularly as I can taste the chorizo on his tongue when he forces it into my mouth.

I don't like this kind of kissing. However, Carlos is not to be deterred. He starts to fiddle with my clothes, slips his hand under my sweater, squeezes each of my breasts, and then slides his hand down my track pants. The next moment I can feel his finger moving around inside of me. Before I realise what is happening, he has unzipped his pants, dived on top of me with his penis in his hand and is thrusting it at my vagina. He doesn't have much success as it is one hell of a squash in the front seat, Fiat 500s not being designed for this activity. He has also caught me completely off guard. I panic and my muscles seize up. I am terrified I'll get pregnant like my best friend back in Australia did, the very first time she had sex. I am also scared witless that someone will come and peer inside our car. Generalissimo Franco runs a tight regime in Spain. Just recently a young couple was arrested and fined for kissing in public! We will surely end up in the clinker if we get caught for this little lot. I feel a flood of warm fluid running down my leg, which smells sickly sweet. When I look down, blood is pouring out of me all over the place.

The doctor's surgery is gloomy—high ceilings, dark painted walls, shelves filled with books and sombre paintings. The doctor's face matches his rooms. He is Carlos's mother's doctor. If she ever finds out about this little excursion, I will really take a dive in her opinion. The doctor, it seems, is not impressed with the situation either. Look what happens to girls who have sex before they are married, his eyes tell me, before he explains that the skin inside my vagina has torn and will require several stitches. Hell! I am sitting on his bench with my legs splayed, blood still pouring out and tears flooding down my face, getting stitched in a place I never could have imagined possible.

Days later I am still distraught. I feel so humiliated and can't stop crying. Carlos tries to comfort me but I am inconsolable. It's like the bottom has fallen out of my world. My emotions are all over the place. We talk long into the night about what I ought to do. Carlos thinks that I should go back to Australia to be with my family for a while. He tells me that he loves me and wants to marry me but has to finish his studies first. He still has a couple of years to go. I am not ready to go home yet or to contemplate marriage, for that matter, but I don't say anything. In the end, I decide to go to England for a while. Bob Howe from Dunlop's has sent me a letter inviting me to play in a few tournaments in the south of England.

Before I leave, Carlos gives me a small gold ring to wear and tells me we're engaged. Are we? I feel funny. I certainly don't feel gay and happy like I imagine a newly engaged girl is supposed to feel. It is hard to describe how I feel exactly. Unsettled is as close as I can come—very unsettled. But it is more than that. I've always felt a certain amount of pressure about getting married. If I don't, something dreadful will happen. I am 21 already and know I am skating close to the "deadline". I'll be left on the shelf if I'm not careful. Most of the girls I know back home got engaged on their 21st birthday at the very latest. Getting married is what I am supposed to do, and I know that Mum and Dad would approve of Carlos.

I let things slide.

But I've always dreamed of something different! Seeing a stranger across a crowded room and falling instantly in love with him at first sight like in *South Pacific*. Although I didn't know it at the time, as the term wasn't invented until 1987, I had a Cinderella complex and was suffering from gender panic.

Fortunately, I manage to get my equilibrium back after a couple of weeks playing in tournaments in the south of England. I play in three tournaments in Devon, supposedly the Mediterranean of England, but the weather certainly doesn't live up to this reputation, especially in Torquay where it rains all week. I spend more time in the dingy, damp, dismal guesthouse and the club house than on the court. As the wet weather sets in our matches are transferred from grass to loam then cement. We play the finals indoor on boards at the Palace Hotel where I win a long and tortuous match, 14–12 in the third set against an English player, Judy Congdon. But only just. In the second set I lose concentration (and the set) when

I start mentally spending the ten pounds prize money on offer on a gorgeous new dress I've seen in the village. I win both the singles and doubles with Vicki Lancaster at Exmouth and Budleigh Salterton, where we are billeted with Vice-Colonel and Mrs Hudson. The colonel, who is a lovely man but a frightful snob, confides in us that they only allow professional or ex-military people to be members of the tennis club. No one in trade, he says with his nose in the air. I tell Mrs Hudson that my mother is a schoolteacher but decide to keep mum about Dad with his electrical appliance business.

Being in an English-speaking country, even though it is very different from Australia, lifts my spirits. There are also a few fellow Australians playing, which helps. I meet up with another Australian girl, Robyn Murphy, who is also going to stay over in Europe for the winter. She decides to come back to Madrid with me.

I'm still miserable

I open my bedroom window wide. I don't care that it's winter. An icy wind whistles through the blinds, scattering my homework over the desk. I haven't done it. Nor am I going to. I can't concentrate. I get into bed, snuggle down underneath the covers, pull the blanket over my head and listen to the radio. At times I almost succeed in shushing the voices inside my head. I hurt all over. My heart aches worst of all. I can't tell anyone what's happened so I pour all my troubles out to my cat, Snow Boots. She looks at me with her green eyes, listens carefully, then snuggles up to me and purrs. I clutch my teddy tight all night. When I wake up he's damp with my tears. I promise myself that I'm never going to be hurt like this again.

Chapter 35

LA MADRE DE CARLOS

On our return Robyn and I are invited for dinner at Carlos's home with his mother. It will be our first meeting, and although Carlos hasn't really said much about her, I've gathered from the little he has divulged that she rules the roost. I am certainly a bit nervous. Memories of how my father used to corner my dates and give them the first degree slither through my mind.

The Fernandez de Cordobas live in Puerta de Hierro, not far from the club, in the only suburb in Madrid I've seen where people live in houses with gardens—huge, beautifully maintained gardens mostly with pools. After ringing the bell, I hardly have time to take a deep breath in a last ditch attempt to settle my nerves, when a maid in a black dress with a white starched apron opens the door. Hovering behind her in the vestibule is an impeccably groomed woman, who is without doubt Senora Fernandez de Cordoba. Standing slightly further back, with a goofy grin on his face, is Carlos.

Senora Fernandez de Cordoba is one of those effortlessly elegant ladies I've seen walking up and down the Calle de Serrano.

Not one of her thick luxuriant hairs is out of place, her perfect olive skin glows in the early evening light and her almond eyes gaze at me superciliously over her slightly raised, faultless Roman nose. As she reaches her perfectly manicured hand towards mine, I want to sink into the floor. My hair is in particularly bad shape tonight. I am still trying to grow it but at the moment it is most definitely at the awkward stage. In a desperate attempt to render it somewhat decent, I've tacked it back with a rubber band and a couple of bobbies. But the side pieces keep popping out. I notice immediately that my jeans, top and Skoll sandals do not meet with Carlos's mother's approval as her eyes move up, then down, then up again. I can almost hear her saying, "Look what the cat's dragged in."

We move from the front entrance into a huge room where a log fire is burning, with comfortable-looking leather chairs and elegant sofas positioned around it. In the far corner, a polished wooden table is set for dinner. I start to get the feeling that it is going to be a long and tedious night. We are shown to our seats and to my dismay I find that I am placed right next to the senora. If she hasn't noticed my nails when we shook hands, now she is bound to. They are, as usual, a disaster. It's not my fault that I have a huge space between the nail and my finger, which always manages to collect dirt. And unfortunately on this particular occasion I haven't had the time to remedy the situation.

No sooner are we seated than another maid serves the first course of *guissantes* and *jamon* (peas with ham). I am just about to lift my knife and fork when I notice that Senora Fernandez de Cordoba has her head bowed. Grace! It doesn't take long for me to discover she definitely has taken a leaf out of my father's book. No sooner does she finish grace than she begins to grill me about everything. What city do I live in? What kind of work does my father do? What education do I have? What religion am I? In no time at all she has found out that I am an uneducated Protestant from Narrabeen with a father in "trade". She is not impressed. On the other hand, she discovers that Robyn, my doubles partner, is a Catholic legal secretary so she turns her back on me and spends the rest of the night talking to her. In one way I am relieved because at least I can eat my peas, which are tricky at the best of times, in peace. I squash them on the back of my fork as I have been taught. Then I watch as both Carlos and his mother turn their forks around and scoop theirs up. Mum and Dad wouldn't be impressed.

I don't miss one

I drag myself out of bed into my tennis clothes then stagger downstairs to the court. Dad coaches me now. He's waiting with two buckets full of balls. He doesn't seem to notice there's anything wrong. This morning we're doing short forehands. Dad half lobs the ball into the service court. I move forward, take my racket back. When the ball reaches the top of its bounce I punch it away for a winner. I hit a hundred balls and don't miss one.

Chapter 36

UNA EXURSION AL CAMPO

When I wake up, it takes several minutes to work out where I am. It is pitch dark. I feel completely disoriented and the rough red wine we drank last night doesn't help. I have no idea what time it is but I am busting to go to the toilet, which I vaguely remember is down the hallway. It is also freezing. I feel my way down the uneven tiled floor then fumble for the long, frayed rope, which turns the light on. Although it feels like the middle of the night, my watch tells me it is well after ten in the morning. The huge old wooden shutters which cover all the windows are stuck closed, stopping even a skerrick of light coming in, so it is always pitch dark inside the old farm house even in the middle of the day. I have slept for more than twelve hours.

I remember yesterday's drive through Cadaques, a small fishing port nestled between a beautiful bay and the mountains, which Carlos told me is renowned as a community for bohemians, intellectuals and artists, in particular Salvador Dali. White stone-washed houses were clustered around the bay, then made their way up narrow stone-paved lanes, their windows bursting with brilliantly coloured flowers and balconies tumbling with lush green vines. We stopped for lunch and a stroll around the bay then walked up Carrer des Call to look for Dali's old home, before proceeding through olive fields and rather untamed countryside to Carlos's parents' holiday farm near the village of Tordera.

Carlos, Robyn and I have come to spend a few days here. I am bored. There is nothing to do after dinner. We are miles from anywhere and there isn't a television, or even a radio to listen to. Not that it would have been much good because my Spanish is still a "work in progress" and Robyn's is non-existent. Carlos gets really pissed off when Robyn and I keep playing "Grooving on a Sunday afternoon" on my cheap little plastic record player which, to be fair, does have the most atrocious sound. But it is better than absolute silence and inactivity which always succeed in making me feel anxious.

No doubt, poor Carlos had envisaged more romantic scenarios but these are a bit hard to implement with Robyn in attendance. She hadn't wanted to stay in Madrid by herself, and Carlos certainly isn't too pleased that she's come. I'm sure he was hoping to be alone with me. We all ended up going to bed early.

Now I'm awake, I'm starving. The dinner the previous evening, that Robyn and I prepared, was a disaster. We insisted on cooking the huge, vibrantly yellow cobs of corn we'd picked out of the garden, despite Carlos's insistence that they were only for the animals. Much to our annoyance, he was right. Even after quite a stretch in the pot, they were as hard as a rock and totally inedible. We'd had to make do with a couple of slices of bread and a few glasses of an ancient-looking bottle of red wine we found in one of the cupboards—hence the foggy head and the beginnings of a headache.

I'm invincible

I'm up 4–3. Dad's umpiring. John and I are very evenly matched. But I know I can beat him if I "shit stir" him. "How many doubles are you going to serve?" I ask as he gets ready to serve. He serves three. I'm up 5–3. John's next shot drops close to the line but is definitely out. Dad says "Play two." I am furious at his interference. I insist that the ball was out and tell him to shut up. As soon as the words escape my mouth I know I've gone too far. Dad leaps off the stand, his old Maxply racquet in hand. I panic and race for the gate. Unfortunately, I fumble with the latch. Dad whacks me a beauty. I wear the marks of the strings on my bottom for the next couple of weeks.

Chapter 37

CASABLANCA

Back in Madrid, Robyn and I are just about to head off to play in a couple of tournaments in Rodos and Thessalonika in Greece. I'd written to them requesting an invitation before I left for England. The offerings proffered by the tournament committee are meagre and only include full hospitality *while we are still playing in the tournament* with no contribution towards our fares to get there. At the last moment we receive an invitation offering a much better deal to play in Casablanca, forwarded to us by good old Bob Howe from Dunlop's. They offer to pay us $500 each to play, plus airfares and full hospitality. It is a fortune, the most I've ever been paid as appearance money. And the opportunity to go to Casablanca— *Casablanca* is one of my favourite movies! It's way too good to resist.

The driver, who picks us up at Casablanca airport, is dark and swarthy. He has a very long, wiry beard sprinkled with grey and the little fingernail on his right hand is so long that it curls around at the end. Dressed in long white flowing robes, with his head covered by a large white cloth tied with a bandana, he looks like he's just stepped out of a scene from *Lawrence of Arabia.*

As we drive away from the airport, the weather is still very warm, although it is mid-autumn. A dusty, dry wind is blowing, and only a few spikelets of desert flowers and shrubs interrupt the flat sandy plains on each side of the road connecting the airport to Casablanca. On the way to the hotel, we pass through the centre of Casablanca, a jungle of cement boxes with slit windows and rusted balconies connected to the electrical supply by a multitude of dodgy-looking frayed cables. This agglomeration is interspersed with the magnificent, intricately decorated facades of mosques and public buildings, oases of palms and waterfalls, gardens bursting with brilliantly coloured flowers, and radiant displays of figs, dates and fruit in market stalls. But it is the people I can't take my eyes off, as they walk up and down the street. They are truly from another world. Only a few of the men are wearing business suits. Most are dressed in a similar manner to our driver, and many have scabbards on low-slung belts. The few women we see are covered from head to toe in swathes of fabric.

As we approach the impressive entrance of Le Royal Mansour Hotel, its white façade glistens in the morning sun. When we step inside, it is as though we are entering a rainforest. We are enveloped by a forest of lush, green, shiny-leafed plants. Nearby, a waterfall cascades down a side wall into a rock pond where large orange fish swim up and down. Shiny, black marble floors connect the entrance to the reception. The ceiling towers up into a high dome window through which the dazzling morning sunlight spotlights a huge chandelier, hanging in the centre of the space. In the far corner, a bearded old man is belting out his repertoire of classical Russian pieces on a violin. In my jeans and t-shirt once again I feel somewhat underdressed.

After we check in, a small boy, who can't be more than about seven and is dressed like a genie, beckons us to follow him to our room. It is huge and opulent. Shiny, embroidered silks and brocades cover the beds and chairs. Gold tassels hang from their corners. The wooden bedsteads and coffee tables are intricately carved. A miniature version of the chandelier downstairs hangs from the centre of the ceiling. When I remove my Scholl sandals, my feet sink into thick, lush Persian rugs. Floating in the loo water in the magnificent marble bathroom I discover rose petals, their delicate fragrance pervading the bathroom. I am in heaven.

Halfway through the week, the players and tournament committee are invited to a celebratory dinner. I overhear the committee members, who are mostly French, complaining bitterly because it is being held at the president of the tennis club's home. As he is a Muslim, much to their annoyance, no wine is going to be served with the food, only almond milk. Such a shame, they lament, to have beautiful food without any wine.

The President's opulent home is encircled by magnificent gardens. On our arrival, we are shown into a large room, furnished with a dozen very low, round tables surrounded by plump, brightly coloured cushions on the floor. I am seated next to a large, important-looking Arab, who sits cross-legged on an overstuffed orange cushion, his stomach resting on his knees. I can't help but notice that he too has a very long fingernail just like the taxi drivers. A huge steaming dish of food is placed in the middle of the table. My neighbour elbows me in the side then volunteers in deep, raspy, heavily accented English that it is couscous, before digging in with his fingers. He then offers his next handful to me. I accept gracefully because he doesn't look like the type of bloke who is used to being knocked back. Besides, I am starving as usual and there are no knives and forks around. I just hope he's cleans that long nail thoroughly and on a regular basis so I don't die of something awful.

We don't speak much because dish after dish of food is constantly being delivered, eaten and removed. Fortunately, my neighbour is much too engrossed in the exercise of eating to indulge in idle chat. I am glad because I am at a loss as to what to talk about. I don't want to offend this big Arab man, as all the other people at the table seem to treat him in a very deferential manner. Another Caucasian woman is sitting on my left. She turns out to be an Australian too, but her appearance is deceiving. She is dressed in the full regalia of an Arab wife, complete with a veil covering most of her face. She whispers her story to me whenever the big Arab is looking the other way, concentrating on his eating, or swigging almond milk. She tells me how she fell in love with a handsome Arab and married him. But now he's taken a younger, second wife and she has been relegated to a very inferior position in the household. She is rarely allowed out of the compound where she lives, except when her husband needs her to speak English. She wants desperately to leave but is absolutely stuck.

"He would kill me if he thought I would even consider leaving him," she confides.

Lucky my penchant for dark-skinned men doesn't extend to Arabs!

At the end of the week, just as we are about to book our plane tickets back to Madrid, Robyn receives a message that her father is desperately ill and has to return to Australia post haste. I am glad to be leaving Casablanca and figure we are lucky to get out unscathed. Robyn, who is an inveterate shopper, has been at the souk across the road from our hotel all week, beating the prices down on rugs and kilims just for the fun of it. She still hasn't bought anything. Although bargaining is almost obligatory, she certainly has taken it to the nth degree. Some of the Jewish and Arab shop vendors were getting very heated under the collar. As most of them wear scabbards I was concerned that we were going to come to grief any minute.

It seems that my doubles partners are falling like flies. I return to Madrid by myself. I am on my own again. Carlos will be pleased.

My first smoke

I'm behind the Nabaren tennis club house with Frosty. He asks if I smoke. "Of course," I reply. He hands me one of his Craven A cork tips then offers me a lighted match. I draw the smoke in and start to cough. My head feels dizzy. Frosty offers to show me how to do the drawback. But I feel sick and my mouth tastes like a dead rat. I think I've had enough smoking for the time being. But I won't give up. I'll practise the drawback on the quiet.

Chapter 38

EL CLUB DE CAMPO

On my return to Madrid, Juan Manuel Couder, the president of the Castillian Tennis Federation, rings to advise that they have decided to offer me a contract for six months to coach the top junior girls. The downside is that I will also have to run classes for beginners on Saturday and Sunday mornings at the Club de Campo. But they offer to pay me 30,000 pesetas a month. That is big bucks! Carlos is slightly miffed. He tells me that he will only earn 12.000 pesetas a month when he graduates in economics.

I decide to lease a serviced apartment just off the Calle de Serrano, instead of staying on with the senora. As much as I love her, she does tend to be a bit overpowering as well as a tad too nosey. I suppose it has been largely my fault as I've confided in her frequently, particularly about my doubts as to whether Carlos was Mr Right. I've also told her about the handsome stranger that I'd encountered over the past couple of years. Her opinion is very similar to what Mum and Dad's would no doubt be. She constantly reiterates that Carlos is excellent husband material. He is from a very "good" family with a home in Puerta de Hierro, one of the most exclusive suburbs in Madrid, will no doubt end up with a university degree in the next couple of years and a good job. Her opinion is that he is eminently suitable and that I should forget any fly-by-night handsome men in cafes and railway stations who'd be nothing but trouble.

Although I will miss the senora, I won't be all that far away. And much to my delight, my new home is closer to all my favourite dress shops. What's more, I'll have some money to spend.

On the first day coaching the junior girls, Juan Couder organises for me to be picked up by Mr Alvarez-Mon, the father of two of the squad members. At first sight, I can see that Mr Alvarez-Mon is not one of the run-of-the-mill, serious, self-important Spaniards with whom I generally cross paths. When he gets out of a rather battered old Range Rover with his hand out ready to shake mine, he is wild-eyed and giggling. I hope that this is a good sign and that he isn't going to be one of those desperate parents who hang on every shot their child makes. However, these personality characteristics unfortunately transfer to his driving. I have to cling to the strap above the door as he drives full bore across the city to the Club de Campo, furiously changing lanes without putting on his blinker, nor checking the traffic behind, while continually turning his head right around to talk to me.

When I arrive, I have to take some deep breaths to calm my nerves before I make my exit from the car. The two sisters, Teresa and Monica, and the third member of the squad, Marianna, turn out to be very nice girls as well as dead keen. When we hit up, I find that they are also reasonable players, particularly Monica. This is great because it means that I can do a lot of work-outs with them instead of the basics, which I always find tedious.

We spend the afternoon doing all the exercises that my tennis coach, Sid Drake, used to give us as kids. As well as the usual cross-court and down-the-line drives, I hit them short balls so they can practise doing approach shots and coming into the net to volley. We also do lots of volleying and smashing exercises, not something that Spanish coaches would have in their repertoire at that time, which they love. We finish up by playing a couple of sets.

Mr Alvarez-Mon is even more wild-eyed and giggly on the way home, having spent the afternoon in the bar. He drives at a death-defying pace, waving one hand around while he talks, and constantly looking around to the back, to make sure he is keeping his audience. I am very relieved when I arrive home and get out somewhat shaken, but still in one piece.

My first period

It happens today. What Annette said. I start bleeding. Not much. There are just a few spots on my pants. They are more brown than red. I have a pain in my tummy too. When I get home from school I tell Mum. She gets out one of those brown paper bags and gives me one of her Modesses. She also gives me a very strange contraption, a piece of elastic which has two strips coming off it with safety pins at the end. She gives me a piece of paper with the instructions and tells me to put it on. I go into the bedroom and lock the door. I'm always hopeless at instructions. It takes me ages to work out what to do. I start to cry. I don't want to get my periods.

Chapter 39

SENOR ROGELIO

It is a perfect autumn day. There is just a touch of freshness in the air and the leaves of the trees down the centre of the Paseo de La Castilliana are just starting to turn gold as I drive out of Madrid mid-afternoon. I've been invited to play in an exhibition tournament with Anna Maria Estelella, the Spanish champion, in Barcelona and am leaving a day early so I can break the trip halfway. I have arranged to have the week off and am looking forward to a break away from the tedium of coaching.

Just as it is starting to get dark, I arrive at an ancient town called Calatayud and begin to look for somewhere to stay. Midway through town, on the left hand side of the road, I notice a plump man who is dressed in an immaculate black suit with a white apron that is starched to within an inch of its life. He is standing in the doorway of an establishment called Senor Rogelio's Restaurante and Pensione, smiling and greeting everyone who passes by.

I pull over to the kerb, hop out and peek through the window into a room which is so dark inside that it looks like it is already well into the night. However, even in the dim light I can see that the serviettes are starched and brilliant white, the glasses glisten, the wooden floor shines and there are bottles of dark ruby red wine already on the tables. The man from the doorway hurries towards me.

"Buenas dias, senorita".

His smiling face radiates such happiness that I automatically smile back and decide immediately that I will stay. Senor Rogelio's smile becomes wider when, after further discussion, he discovers that I am going to *dormir* (sleep) as well as *comer* (eat). He shows me upstairs to a large room with a rather suspect looking bed in it. The bathroom, he tells me, is down the end of the hall, not my favourite place for bathrooms. However, it is very cheap and includes dinner and breakfast. I shake hands with him and return downstairs to the restaurant.

The large bottle of red wine on my table, according to the label, comes from Mr Rogelio's own vineyard. When I pour some into my glass and take a sip, it is big and bold, just how I like it. As is the custom in Spain, my meal is some time coming but when it arrives it also is very good. The waiter who serves me tells me in a confidential tone that Senor Rogelio has won El Gordo (the lottery) and has built himself a huge home outside town with its own vineyard. No wonder he is smiling at everyone. I am glad that I only have to go upstairs after dinner, even if the bed is not going to be all that comfortable. After half a bottle of Senor Rogelio's wine, most of it having been consumed before eating, I can hardly keep my eyes open. I flop on the bed and am instantly dead to the world.

Surprisingly enough it turns out to be one of the best night's sleep I'd ever had, despite the bed. After breakfast the following morning, Senor Rogelio is there to wave me off.

"Hasta la vista, Senorita Susana," he cries, as I take off down the street to Barcelona. "*Espero que vuelva Usted pronto*!" (I hope to see you again soon.)

Anna Maria Estelella and I are playing an exhibition match for the opening of a new, very exclusive club. Once again I win even though I have a terrible bout of bronchitis and have to wheeze my way around the court. I imagine in another life Anna Maria would have been a nun. She is always so calm, cool and collected and never seems to get the least bit upset that I always beat her.

All aboard

Mum and Dad are going to England on the Queen Mary. *During the afternoon, we go and see* West Side Story. *It's the first musical I've ever seen and I love every minute of it. I can hardly stop myself from dancing my way down the street. In the early evening we go aboard to look at their cabin until the loudspeaker booms. "We're preparing to sail in half an hour. All visitors aboard must now disembark." We race down the gangplank, waving our last goodbyes. I can hardly wait to get home. Mrs Mac, my eldest sister's mother-in-law, is looking after us. I've quite a few things I want to do while Mum and Dad are away. I've got my eye on Mrs Mac's Magic Silver White that she uses to colour her hair.*

The instructions on the side of the bottle advise two drops but I decide two aren't anywhere near enough. Fourteen will do the trick. I tip it on my hair then rinse it out. When I look in the mirror my hair has gone a bright and luminous purple. I'm in deep shit! I shampoo my hair six times. It's still very, very purple. Lucky it's school holidays. I tie one of Mum's old scarves around my head and light a cigarette. I have my very own packet of Capstan now and can nearly do the drawback.

Chapter 40

El RELAMPAGO

I always love getting back to Madrid, even though on this particular occasion the weather is every bit as contrary as it is elsewhere in the world during the change of seasons. I arrive on the most beautiful sunny day. The next day the rain is absolutely pissing down, so my tennis coaching is transferred indoors to the Club Chamartin. I don't mind at all really. Chamartin is just around the corner from my place so I don't have to risk life and limb driving across town with Senor Alvarez-Mon. And, although I really like the Club de Campo, which is situated on the outskirts of Madrid and has its own polo fields and golf course, I much prefer Club Chamartin. With its indoor and outdoor courts, pool, gym, sauna and luxuriously appointed bars and restaurants it is definitely something to write home about.

It certainly leaves the tennis centres I grew up playing at in Australia for dead, with their tin sheds at the side of each court, where we sat on long hot Saturday afternoons between sets, consuming endless cups of sugary tea and pikelets, jam and cream. At Chamartin, smartly dressed, black-aproned waiters bustle between tables, carrying silver trays and serving people elegant morsels on fine china with sparkling, silver cutlery.

On my first day coaching at Chamartin, as I walk towards the ladies' change rooms, I pass the most gorgeous man. It takes me a second before I realise it is the very one I'd seen at the Café Gijon and then again at Atocha Station. I can't believe my luck! I have to *force* myself not to stop in my tracks and *stare*. He is just as stunningly handsome as I remember. Dark and very tall for a Spaniard, with gleaming skin, shining, thick wavy luxurious hair and glistening teeth, his full lips gently curve into the most amazing smile which literally lights up the whole hallway.

And believe it or not, he is dressed for tennis, racquet in hand. What an amazing coincidence! I never dreamt that I would see him again. "Who is *that*?" I whisper to the girls in my squad, who shake their heads then shrug. I will be playing in a tournament at Chamartin next week and fervently hope that he will be around.

As I enter the club on the first day of the tournament, I spot him. What an incredibly lucky break! Ever resourceful, in the meantime I've found out that his name is Pedro Riviera de Flores. Today he looks even more gorgeous than ever, dressed in a suit. I can't take my eyes off him and spend the whole day positioning myself so I can check him out. When he moves to the far side of the stands around the centre court, I sneak underneath and casually appear to be arriving from the other direction. When he goes towards the club house, I whip around to the rear entrance, come in by the back door and then casually stroll towards the front of the club.

Each time I see him, he smiles at me. My heart beats so loudly in my chest, I am afraid he will notice something.

I blush from top to toe, my stomach feels like it is somewhere around my knees, and as for my knees, they are so pumped with adrenalin that they feel like they have disappeared altogether. I feel like I'm walking around without them. At last I know what Mum and Aunty Nena were talking about all those years ago when I'd quizzed them over that afternoon tea about how I would I know when I met Mr Right. They had answered that I would "just know". And now I do. Poor Carlos! In my heart of hearts, I've always known he wasn't "the one" and this fateful meeting has confirmed it.

By the end of the week I am absolutely exhausted by all the extra running around I've been doing, off as well as on the court. My emotions are running wild and I've hardly been able to sleep a wink. After the tournament finishes and I have to get back to my normal routine, I find it almost impossible to concentrate on anything. All I can think about is Pedro. Worst of all, I don't even know if I will ever see him again as we don't play at Chamartin all that often. The members there aren't too keen on letting non-members use their courts; they like to have them for themselves even if they are empty. And I don't really blame them. I've heard that the membership fee is $10,000, which is an absolute fortune in Spain, and the members have to pay exorbitant quarterly levies as well.

A couple of mornings later someone calls me. I'm not sure who's speaking so rapidly and in such a confidential tone. It is a man, asking me out. I knock him back, thinking that it is the twerp from down the street, who's been plaguing me ever since I moved here. Although my Spanish is improving, I still can't really understand all that well on the phone and tend to panic. It isn't until I put the receiver down that it dawns on me that it might be Pedro. But how did he get my number? Will he ever call me again after such discouragement?

It *is* Pedro. And thank God he does call again. He asks me out for dinner the next day. But I am ready!

"Lunch," I say.

I've been thinking things over and am a bit nervous about going out at night with someone who, in reality, I don't really know at all. At least in daylight, I will feel safer, especially if things don't work out and I have to make a quick getaway. What I am going to wear is the next question. I spend the next couple of hours trying on everything in my wardrobe. Nothing is suitable for such a special occasion so I go out and buy a gorgeous new outfit at my favourite boutique on Serrano.

Pedro picks me up just before lunch in a gleaming dark green car.

"It's a Mustang Mach 11," he informs me. "There are only two of them in Spain. The other one belongs to Juan Carlos, el Principe."

Unlike my brother, I am not a car person so am not the least bit impressed about this piece of news. All I can think about is how incredibly handsome Pedro is. It is not only his good looks; he is also immaculately groomed and, once again, he is wearing a beautiful suit. There is also something special about him, a certain enigmatic magnetism that he has, an aura. And it isn't just me who notices it. People in the street turn and stare at him as he comes around to the passenger side of the car to open the door for me. I am totally flummoxed and move towards the car as though I am in a dream. I really don't know how I manage to get in and sit down without incident. My chest feels so tight I can hardly breathe and once again my knees have totally deserted me. In fact, they have gone wobbly, causing me to feel decidedly unsteady on my feet.

A very pompous-looking, impeccably uniformed doorman, who greets Pedro by his name (prefixed by the honorific don), meets us at the door of L'hardy. The restaurant is upstairs, which I find somewhat difficult to manage with my jelly knees. When I step inside I can see Pedro has chosen an extremely opulent restaurant for lunch. As the maitre d' leads us to our table, I look around the dimly lit interior. Sombre dark wooden furniture, polished to within an inch of its life, has been meticulously placed around the room and against the embossed leather-covered walls. Thick crimson velvet curtains are draped over the windows and as I move forward, the plush ruby carpet sinks beneath my step. Although it is the middle of the day, it is as though it has become the night, which is fortuitous. With a bit of luck Pedro won't be able to notice how nervous I am.

I breathe deeply to steady myself. But I still can't feel my knees until we sit down opposite each other and our knees touch accidentally. Suddenly they have returned. It is like an electrical charge shooting through my body. I am so sexually attracted to Pedro, I feel like I could jump right over the table, then and there. It is wild! And a worry! I haven't had sexual feelings like this since those long ago passionate encounters I experienced with my tennis coach. Halfway through lunch, when Pedro places his hand briefly over mine, my whole body feels like it is on fire. My throat constricts to such an extent I can hardly get a morsel down. In this bedazzled state, I sip my glass of delicious Marques de Riscal carefully. I am not much of a drinker, and would hate to make a fool of myself in this posh establishment, especially in front of such a gorgeous creature.

The meal goes by in a haze. Pedro does most of the talking, because as well as having difficulty in swallowing my food, I am also, although all my friends would find it impossible to believe, stuck for words. All I know is that I am totally captivated by every word Pedro utters and everything he does. His line of chat is so much more interesting than that of the boys I have dated in Australia. I can't take my eyes off him. He is just so gorgeous. Even his hands are beautiful. His long slim fingers move gracefully while he eats, elegantly dunking his bread in the sauce.

Pedro starts off by telling me about how he grew up in a small village called Veneros, which is about twenty kilometres across country along a rough bush track from the nearest town, Bonar, in the province of Leon.

"Veneros is situated in a valley at the foot of the Picos de Europa, which are covered in snow from the middle of September until May. Due to its inaccessibility because of the mountainous terrain, this area has never been invaded by anyone since the Vizigodos. My family are direct descendants of King Rodrigo, the last king of the Goths," he tells me.

"Our family was once very wealthy and we lived in a huge mansion in grand style in Leon, but my grandfather lost everything except for a small finca in Veneros, one night in a card game. That finca is the family home, where I grew up. It's a two-storey white stucco building with only shutters for windows. During most of the year, because it was so cold, the farm animals lived underneath. There was no electricity. Nor was there running water in any of the houses. The villagers had to rely on a fast flowing mountain stream at the top end of town for their household needs and washing. But in springtime, Veneros is a wondrous place and very beautiful," Pedro continued. "Behind the village, the hillsides are covered in vibrantly coloured yellow and purple flowers, the sky is cobalt blue and snow-capped mountains can be seen in the distance."

I find it hard to imagine that this beautifully dressed, sophisticated man comes from such a basic background. I hang on with bated breath as he goes on to tell me about his childhood—how he left home when he was only eleven, after an argument with his father, and went to live in Bilbao all by himself, where he worked on the docks.

He told me he'd learned fast, grew up quick and was involved in many wild, exciting and sometimes reckless schemes and adventures. Later on he built up a substantial business which he tried unsuccessfully to turn into a cooperative, but the workers took over and ousted him as the director, so he moved to Madrid.

He went on to say that these days he is a successful businessman and makes his living mostly by importing pearls from Japan. He has managed to secure one of only five permits and, as Generalissimo Franco's wife wears pearls, it is almost a licence to print money.

"It is every Spanish woman's dream to own a strand of cultured pearls," he continues. "Fortunately, this work doesn't take up too much of my time. I have a partner, Bruno, in Tokyo who buys all the pearls and ships them over to me. All I have to do is get them through customs, then deliver them to the wholesalers and collect the money. I spend the rest of my time pursuing my other interests. I research and invest in the stock market, which involves going to the stock exchange most mornings. In the afternoons, I paint and am learning English."

English? He must only just have started his lessons because his English is atrocious.

He tells me that he also loves to cook, eat and drink wine, but unfortunately he has recently been diagnosed with stomach ulcers. His doctor has advised him to change to a blander, low-fat diet and do more exercise. And that's why he has joined the Chamartin Tennis Club.

"Even though the membership is expensive," he says, "because it is in the form of a re-saleable share, and there are always lots of people on the waiting list wanting to buy in, I am not too concerned. If I decide I don't like tennis, I will probably make a profit."

Once again I don't know what to say.

Although Mum always used to tell me that it was best to have "things in common" with a partner, that always seemed so boring to me. I much prefer differences. Even though she warned me that while opposites attract, quite often in her experience it doesn't work out. She was always quoting an old family adage: "When Cupid draws back the string of his bow, nobody knows where the arrow will go." She'd been talking about her sister Nena, who'd fallen in love and married a handsome soldier from Perth. The family had been very much against the liaison but there was no stopping Nena. However, after having three children things went drastically downhill. With Dad's assistance, Nena ended up making an escape back to Sydney.

Pedro goes on to tell me how he would never forget the first time he saw me at the Club Chamartin when I was coaching the young girls, and then the following week at the tournament.

"It seemed that everywhere I looked you were there, like an angel. I fell in love with you straight away."

If someone came up with this line in English, I decide, it would sound absolutely absurd. But in Spanish it is another story. It sounds incredibly romantic. Luckily Pedro has no idea of the "back and forth under the stand" tactics I'd employed to attract his attention. Somehow I manage to stifle my giggles when I start thinking about it, although I nearly burst in the process and have to repair to the ladies' post haste.

I ponder what I am going to do about Carlos and our engagement, while I twist the small gold ring he's given me around and around. Then I start to wonder how old Pedro is. He certainly seems to have done so much in his life that he must be at least 30. I try to think of other people I know and how old they are to compare. I don't dare ask. That would be just too gauche for words!

I'm in the doghouse

I'm sitting outside the headmistress's office. A classmate has been caught reading one of the books I found outside an old house on the corner of Pittwater Road and Wetherill Street in Collaroy. It's a real sizzler, called Strike Heaven in the Face. *The teacher writes a note for the headmistress then sends me to sit outside her office. "I'm not impressed with your selection of literature," Miss Fredericks, the headmistress tells me. "Your sister, Annette is a prefect and her behaviour is always exemplary." She sends the book home with Annette. Mum isn't too impressed either. She puts it in the bin. I get it out and read it!*

Chapter 41

UNA PROPUESTA DE MATRIMONIO

I now know what people mean when they say that time went by in a flash. I feel like I am living with the fast-forward button pressed when towards the end of that very first lunch, over coffee, Pedro asks if I would come and live with him. Whoa there! Who me? My mind goes instantly into wild raptures with the possibility of sharing every day of my life with such a beautiful creature. Then into turmoil. Does he really want to live with me? He doesn't know me at all, really. Just over lunch and I've hardly said a word. Anyway, nobody I know lives with anyone unless they're married. It is just not the *done* thing. And what would happen if I got pregnant? Dad would definitely *not* be impressed if I got into the family way *before* I was married.

Once again I don't know what to say. It seems I am always at a loss for words with Pedro. Then I say no, no! I wouldn't live with a man unless I was married to him. And Pedro, without even pausing to take a breath, asks if I will marry him. At that stage, the men in white coats should have most definitely been called. I must be absolutely insane, but the word escapes from my mouth before I can be at all rational. "Yes!" I don't know him either, but I feel so dangerously full of the most incredibly strong feelings and crazy lust for him, I could burst on the spot.

The next day I come plummeting down to earth. There are two things I need to make Pedro aware of before things progress any further. Firstly, I need to show him how I live. I am a grot, which he is no doubt going to find out fairly early in the piece. Housework is not a word which is in my vocabulary. I only do what is absolutely necessary, so except on every second Thursday, when my apartment is serviced, I live in ever-increasing chaos. I don't want Pedro thinking I will make a good housewife as that would be just too far from the truth. He seems to think I am perfect. It is only fair that I enlighten him about this aspect of my personality.

Pedro has insisted on coming today. The cleaner isn't due at my flat until tomorrow so it is at its worst. I can only hope that he won't be put off by my lack of housekeeping skills. What a disaster that would be!

When Pedro arrives, my apartment is in its usual day-thirteen state of chaos and disorder. The last few days of food-encrusted plates and dirty saucepans are overflowing the sink, clothes are strewn on the bed and sofa, and the usual plastic bag with dirty tennis clothes is hanging on the door knob. There is also a rather motley-looking card from Mum and Dad for my 22nd birthday which was just over a month ago. It has been the resting place for many tea and coffee mugs since its arrival.

As Pedro steps inside, my cat, Henrietta, jumps out of the wardrobe where she's been having a snooze in the cardigan drawer. She proceeds to leap from one piece of furniture to another and then, having completed her morning exercise regime, regally minces across the bed and plonks down on the end of it. Nose held high, tail aloft, she inclines her head and inspects Pedro. She then proceeds to give herself an all-over wash. At least she doesn't *ssssst* at him. Funnily enough, Pedro doesn't blink an eye. In fact, he doesn't seem to mind at all. I hope he likes cats.

The other thing I have to inform Pedro about is my engagement to Carlos. *El pobrecito*! Carlos must be wondering where I've disappeared to and what on earth has been going on over the last few days. I hate the thought of having to break it off with him. I haven't had any luck with "breaking up" on either side of the equation. I am a gutless wonder when it comes to difficult situations. All I ever want do is to crawl into a shell and disappear, the ostrich method, hoping fervently that the situation will resolve itself and blow over without me having to do anything.

So, when Pedro tells me he will do the "dirty deed" for me, a load is immediately lifted from my shoulders. It is definitely the coward's way out but I am only momentarily ashamed and very relieved. So I thankfully agree.

Over the rest of the week, when I'm not coaching, Pedro and I spend every free moment together. He doesn't even attend to his investments at the stock market. We sit in restaurants, and between meals, in the car. We have the most amazing and illuminating conversations, while trying to keep our hands to ourselves and behaving respectfully. I continually feel like tearing his clothes off and leaping on top of him but I have to be careful. I also must be discreet. I can't go to his place even in the daytime because if anyone saw me I'd lose my job immediately.

The Stomp

*When Wyeth and I arrive at the North Narrabeen Surf Club
for the Stomp, there are heaps of old panel vans, kombies
and utes in the carpark, filled with surfboards and boys
drinking beer. Couples are huddled together on the beach.
We are supposed to be at the movies. "Feel like a beer, love?"
a bloke yells as we scurry up the stairs. Once inside, we stand
up the front near the band. The room's packed. The people
dancing are older than us. No one asks us to dance. But we
don't care. We just like being here, listening to the music.
And later on we dance with each other.*

Chapter 42

LA BODA

Pedro arranges for a judge from Leon (which is near where he grew up) to marry us in a civil ceremony because I'm not a Catholic. I am getting very nervous about my decision to marry him in such haste but I can't see any alternative. I'm worried I won't be able to hold out too much longer before I give in to his sexual demands. I have such a strong sexual attraction to him. I don't want to get pregnant outside of marriage like my best friend. Apart from the fact that he seems just so perfect in every way!

When the wedding takes place a few days later, I wear the most beautiful long, cream silk dress and pale aqua coat with diamante buttons. It is the most gorgeous dress I've ever owned. Most brides I've known feel rushed off their feet with six or twelve months to plan their weddings. I do it in less than a week as I need to fit it in around work. I don't want to let anyone know I am getting married. After such a short courtship, everyone's bound to assume I'm pregnant. Not that it is going to be a lavish affair with heaps of guests.

The wedding ceremony doesn't turn out to be the romantic event I'd always dreamed about. I'd always envisioned myself dressed in a beautiful white, full-length flowing gown complete with train, matching satin slippers and net veil, walking proudly down the aisle at St Faiths (the church where I'd sung in the choir in my early teens) on my father's arm, surrounded by friends and family. In fact, it turns out to be a rather dry affair with just one other couple, friends of Pedro's I haven't met before as our witnesses. Pedro won't even let me invite the senora who, needless to say, is devastated.

It takes place in the judge's poky, windowless rooms, where every surface is piled high with files and books. Much to my disappointment, there are no flowers, and no stirring bridal march or familiar words of the wedding service, just a lot of signing of papers written in Spanish. Once outside, Pedro slips an envelope to the two witnesses who hot-foot it down the street and are out of sight in no time.

We go to a newly opened Russian restaurant for our wedding dinner. As we step out of the totally transparent lift, which has sped past I don't know how many floors up the side of the building at break-neck speed, not being one for heights, I feel decidedly woozy. Pedro tells me that he's chosen the restaurant because he is crazy about everything Russian.

"Do you know that only last month Spain opened commercial relations with Russia?" he asks.

Geez, I hope he's not a bloody commo, because Dad is a staunch Liberal voter and would be far from impressed if I've up and married a Red. Then he tells me that he has started studying Russian. Languages are definitely not Pedro's forte so I sincerely hope he has more luck with Russian than he has done so far with English.

I was really looking forward to our wedding dinner, but it also is a big disappointment, a decidedly flat affair. For some reason the conversation is stilted. Maybe the seriousness of the step we've taken in such haste has started to sink in. I've also never tried Russian food before and feel very awkward when I discover I don't like it at all. The meal starts off with black salmon caviar, which smells and tastes like fish that has gone off. This is followed by borsch, which of all things turns out to be *beetroot* soup. Yuck! I hate beetroot. I don't like to think about how many Saturdays I spent as a child sitting at the dining table until I ate my bloody beetroot. Now the Russians have turned it into a soup! The main course, Pedro informs me, is *pelmeni* (meat balls) served with potato cakes smothered with sour cream and very salty cabbage. I can't even console my palate with a nice glass of red wine because the meal is accompanied by double nips of vodka served in bowls of ice by poker-faced Russian waiters. It tastes absolutely revolting, like I imagine poison would taste, burning my throat as it goes down and making me feel dizzy. The Russian coffee which follows is not much better, but I sip it slowly as by this time I am in a state of extreme agitation about what is going to happen *after* dinner.

Pedro carries me over the threshold then dumps me somewhat unceremoniously on the floor just inside the vestibule of his apartment, right under the coat rack. There aren't any sweet words of love whispered in my ear or any loving foreplay. He hurriedly pulls up my dress, almost tears my panties off and leaps on top of me while simultaneously pushing his penis inside of me. After all the bloody build-up it is over in two minutes max, but fortunately without the disastrous repercussions of my previous effort with Carlos.

I certainly am not transported anywhere near heaven, like Lady Chatterley was with her lover. In fact, it is a decidedly earthly and most uncomfortable experience. I only hope that it is just a case of the "nervous Nellies" on both our parts and that our marital relations will improve on further acquaintance. After all the carry-on I've heard about sex over the years there just has to be more to it than this.

The Easter long weekend
MAITLAND

We're staying in a cabin in the camping area during the tournament. I'm in the finals. I play Vi Johnson from Newcastle. She's the Newcastle champion and is a very good player. I beat her 6–2 6–3. At the prize-giving dinner dance, we do the Barn Dance, the Pride of Erin and the Canadian Three Step. I also learn to do the Town Hall Crawl with Mal McIllwaine. We dance two steps to the right, one to the left—everyone moves clockwise around the hall.

Chapter 43

UNA CARTA ESPECIAL

The day after the wedding I receive a letter from Dad.

It is the only one he's written to me since I've been away, so I am a bit surprised. Normally it is Mum who writes to me each week, letting me know what is going on at home.

Dearest Sucat, I am writing to you because I think it is now time that you give some serious consideration to your future. You are after all twenty-two. You've had a wonderful time in Europe over the last few years, but in my mind, now's the time you need to come back home to Australia and settle down. We all love and miss you here. Please think seriously about this. Let me know when you're coming and I will organise your plane ticket back.

Love Dad

Dad must be psychic. I didn't dare let him and Mum know about Pedro and me beforehand because I would have had to face a barrage of questions. But now I'll definitely have to call and let them know.

I lift up the phone then put it down again. I feel nervous and a bit guilty. It is ages since I've written home, let alone rung.

Long distance calls are prohibitively expensive and telephones hard to come by. I have also been distracted lately and I suppose, on the whole, a bit slack. Mum writes to me every week without fail with news of family, friends and general "goings-on", although sometimes I don't receive her aerogrammes until quite some time later. Bob Howe from Dunlop does his best to forward them on but often he doesn't have my address or I'm on the move. My main problem is if I did write home, what would I write about? Mum and Dad would be on the first plane over if I told them what was really going on. And once I let a few weeks slide by, the little news I could have relayed, I've completely forgotten about. Anyway, it would be out of date. A couple of times I've written and then not been able to track down a post office to buy a stamp and end up throwing away the letter because all the news in it is old. Things aren't as straightforward as they are in Australia.

I really would prefer to put ringing up off for a couple of days, but I decide to bite the bullet and get it over with.

"Hi Mum. Just ringing to tell you some good news."

"Hullo darling. This is a lovely surprise. How are you?"

"I'm married! I got married yesterday," I manage to squeeze out.

Mum is certainly a bit taken aback. "To Carlos?" she asks.

I'd forgotten that the last time I wrote to them I was engaged to Carlos!

"No, Pedro."

I update her. Of course, Mum is absolutely thrilled to hear the news as she always loves to hear about people getting married especially if both of the couple are tall. Mum has this thing about height. She thinks that if I marry a short man, I will produce short grandsons which in her mind would be an all-out disaster. It is the first question she asks.

"Is he tall?"

"Six foot one", I reply.

"That's wonderful, darling," she says.

However, I can hear Dad in the background and his reaction is not quite so enthusiastic. In fact, I bet he is cursing up a storm. No doubt he feels that he really shot himself in the foot when he interfered in my relationship with Harry, by insisting I went overseas to play tennis for a year before settling down. Harry had been eminently splendid husband material. Now look what's happened. No doubt, a fate worse than death in Dad's eyes. I've gone and married a Spaniard!

"Give me the phone, Thelma," I hear Dad saying in the background. Always with his eye on the bottom line, Dad's first question is, "Does Pedro have any money?"

I'm not too sure of Pedro's exact financial situation, but I did check out with the *portero* in our building who owns this apartment. He informed me that Pedro does. So I relay this piece of information to Dad. Luckily Pedro's English is so terrible that he can't understand a word that is being said. And just as well because if he did, I am sure he would be far from impressed with his new in-laws wanting to know whether he has any money or not.

When I look back now I realise that I didn't know the difference between love and lust. Or at least I found them hard to separate especially when I was in the thick of things. Well brought-up girls were kept in the dark, about sex in particular. Information was not forthcoming in those days as it was thought it would no doubt lead us astray. I hadn't even heard of the word relationship. On reflection, as I had only known Pedro for such a brief period before getting married, I think it was most definitely a case of *lust*!

Phew. A close shave—very close

Mum and Dad are going around the old house from room to room. Their shoes slide past, a matter of inches from my nose. "Has anyone seen my daughter, Sue?" Dad asks. "Don't know no one called Sue," says a bloke who is as pissed as a fart and has just finished peeing over the balcony. After they leave, I crawl out from under the bed. I'm shaking. Geraldine steps out of the wardrobe. We are at a party and the next-door neighbour has rung Mum and Dad and dobbed us in. We're supposed to be at the movies. We catch the bus into Manly and buy movie tickets. And just as well. Next morning at breakfast there is an inquisition about the movie I saw. Later on I hear that Dad got the manager to turn the lights on at the Collaroy Cinema and was walking up and down the aisles looking for me.

Chapter 44

EL MATRIMONIO

After all the excitement of the past few days I sleep like the dead. When I wake up, for the first few moments, I feel totally disoriented until I turn my gaze to the other side of the bed and look at Pedro. He is still fast asleep. His skin is glowing in the early morning light, his hair glistens and his eye lashes, which are thick and lush, are resting languidly on his cheek. He is a perfect specimen in the looks department, I decide, after giving him another careful examination. I feel my heart beating as my eyes linger on his face and body. I still feel such a strong attraction to him, my whole body feels alive when I'm close to him—I feel like I'm going to burst.

But what am I going to do about the sex part? Is it always going to be like it was on our wedding night? What about those mountains of desire followed by peaks of ecstasy in *Lady Chatterley's Lover*, *Strike Heaven in the Face*, *Under the Bramble Bush* and the other penny-dreadfuls I've read from cover to cover several times?

I try to broach the subject with Pedro on several occasions, but without success.

"If you talk about sex, *mi truchin*, (my little trout)," he says, "you'll take away from '*el espiritual.*"

I don't know about that! I am not exactly sure what he means by 'el espiritual', but there must be more to sex than what has gone on so far, a lot more. Otherwise, how come there was always such a carry-on about it? I wish I had someone to discuss things with.

I get up and make a cup of tea. While I sip it, I practise signing my new name—Senora Susana Alexander-Riviera de Flores. Now that's impressive! As is the huge diamond ring Pedro gave me last night. However, I didn't get to wear it for very long because before we went to bed, he told me I'd be better off keeping it in his safe, if I didn't want to lose my finger.

I wander around Pedro's flat, which is huge and takes up the whole floor of the building although it only has one bedroom. The far wall of the huge living area, which extends from one end of the apartment to the other, has two double doors leading out to an enormous balcony, and is covered with dark wooden cabinets. In front of them is a huge fish tank where one lone, rather large fish is swimming around. Pedro told me yesterday, with a tear in his eye, that there had originally been twenty fish. Unfortunately, this last remaining fish has eaten all the others.

The rest of the walls have a mixture of Pedro's paintings interspersed with English verbs stuck on them. Poor Pedro! He really struggles with English, which I suppose is not surprising. Having left school so young, he is probably not up on nouns, verbs and grammar, which I imagine would make learning another language very difficult, nigh impossible.

I end up back in the vestibule, wincing at the scene of our wedding night's disappointment. Then I open the front door and go up a private staircase situated to the right of the elevator, which I soon discover leads to a beautiful roof garden. This apartment is certainly a lot different to the one-bedroom flats they've just started to build on the Northern Beaches.

Later that morning, when Pedro and I go up to the roof garden, I am wearing my favourite yellow and white polka dot box-pleated mini. He is just a few steps below me. I stop in my tracks when I hear what he says.

"Que ahora que eres una senora, que no debes llevar las faldas tan cortas". (Now that you are a married woman, you can't wear such short skirts.)

Hombre! (Really) I can't believe what I am hearing and burst into fits of giggles. I honestly think he is kidding me, but when I turn to look at him, blow me down if he hasn't got the most serious look on his face. He is deadly earnest—he's not joking!

When I come home in the afternoon and go to hang my jacket in the wardrobe, much to my horror I find that all my clothes have disappeared. In place of my mini-skirts and figure-hugging tops are long dark skirts and high-necked blouses. Senora clothes! I am only 22. In Australia, women don't start to dress in a more matronly fashion until they turn 40. He'll be wanting me to get a perm next and take up golf!

Fortunately, I manage to catch him as he is heading downstairs with a large plastic rubbish bag full of my things and tell him in no uncertain terms to put them right back in the cupboard where he got them from. There is no way he is going to turn me into an old dag just yet!

A few days later, halfway through that morning's "roll in the hay", Pedro tells me that he has decided that he isn't going to climax anymore, because according to one of the books that he is reading, he will lose all his strength. I check out the two books on his bedside table, one about Confucianism and the other Taoism. I'm not sure which one has given these strange recommendations. However, I do find this turn of events very strange. One of the few things we discussed *before* we were married was how we both wanted to have children. And pronto! But how is this ever going to happen if he doesn't shoot the beans? Even I know it takes two to tango when it comes to having babies! And let's face it, I sincerely doubt whether God has chosen me, an Australian tennis player, for the second Virgin birth here in Madrid!

After this little episode, he disappears into the bathroom where he remains for more than an hour. Goodness knows what he gets up to in there, but when he does eventually come out, he certainly looks drop dead gorgeous! I don't know what to do about this situation. I haven't ever lived with a man before, let alone a Spanish man! There isn't anyone here I know well enough to talk to about something like this. I only hope that he'll get sick of this behaviour and the whole thing will blow over.

Secrets

I can hear Mum and Dad talking about me. Dad thinks I'm going through a difficult teenage stage. Mum's worried. She says I won't pass the Intermediate the way things are going. And she's probably right. I came third in sixth class, thirteenth in the half-yearly in first year, then down to 26th at the end of the year. Now halfway through second year, I've come 44th. There are only 45 in the class. I hate school. I can't concentrate. Mum and Dad have no idea what's wrong. What surprises me is that they don't notice that I've had such a sudden change in behaviour. I even look different. But they don't ask me what's up. I know if they did I'd blab. There's no way I would be able to keep a lid on it.

Chapter 45

VAYA QUE DESASTRE

I've been bursting with excitement all morning and can hardly contain myself by the time I finally manage to get Pedro out the door. He lingers, almost as if knowing I am up to something. But he certainly has no idea what. It is Jomey's, the maid's day off today and I've decided I am going to surprise Pedro by spring cleaning the kitchen. Pedro *loves clean*. In fact most surfaces in the apartment would be suitable to perform surgery on. He is going to be so happy when he comes home and sees what a wonderful job I've done. I can imagine him admiring the results of my work, a glistening kitchen, shining pans and, of course, spotless cupboards.

I head for the kitchen, pausing at the door to assess the situation, because I'm not exactly sure where to start. I haven't done much cleaning, nor as I've previously mentioned, have I ever had any interest in it. But I am so madly in love with Pedro that I am prepared to do just about anything to impress him. I don't have any coaching on today and Pedro has already warned me that now I am a senora I'm not to go wandering up and down the street by myself.

When I stop to think back about it, I suppose my lack of housekeeping skills have come about because Mum always let me off the hook as a child. I think she felt sorry for me because I was always so exhausted from playing all that tennis, before and after school. I must admit that I was also fairly cunning. I knew that if I didn't tidy my room, after about three weeks Mum wouldn't be able to bear it any longer, she'd weaken and do it for me. All I would have to do is to hang out when she nagged me. I really don't have much experience at all.

But it can't be all that hard. Anyway, it is going to be an adventure! After a bit more daydreaming about the end result and further consideration, I decide to start by taking everything out of the cupboards. Next I am going to thoroughly clean each item, then wipe out the cupboards and lastly, put everything back. That is my plan. But it definitely doesn't turn out to be as easy as I've imagined. I manage to get everything out of the cupboards all right, but it takes absolutely ages, way longer than I've envisaged. Some of the cupboards are very high up and packed to the rafters. I have to go up and down the kitchen ladder I don't know how many times. It turns out to be a very tedious and boring exercise. Quite often I find myself just floating off into dreamland like I used to at school. Half an hour later, I am still halfway up or down the ladder, saucepan in hand, having to think twice about whether I am going up or down.

The next problem is that there's not much room to work in. In no time at all, the kitchen benches are stacked high, and I have to resort to putting stuff onto the floor. By this stage, I can hardly get into the kitchen. I had no idea that there was so much stuff crammed inside those cupboards. Then I start trying to wash up all the pans which have obviously been gathering dust, for goodness knows how long, up there in the top cupboards. Unfortunately, the dust has coagulated on the still greasy surfaces, and is almost impossible to move without a lot of elbow grease. I've hardly made a dent in things, when I hear the door close. Pedro has come home early from the stock market!

As he peers into the kitchen, disaster reigns. Things I've washed up, but haven't yet gotten around to rinsing the soap suds off (and I've certainly used plenty of detergent to ensure that I get everything really clean) are piled high, and soap suds are spilling out of the sink and bubbling up everywhere. The floor is covered with things waiting to be washed.

"*Que disastre, hombre! Que estas haciendo, Mujer,*" Pedro exclaims. (What a disaster! What on earth are you doing, woman?)

This is definitely not the outcome I'd anticipated. I try to explain, but Pedro, instead of appreciating my efforts and admiring all my hard work, completely does his loll and insists on ringing up Jomey, to get her to come over and remedy the situation. I am devastated and totally humiliated. I feel like a hopeless failure and am so disappointed at the outcome that I burst into tears and head for the bedroom.

A short time later Pedro knocks on the door. He sits down on the edge of the bed. "You don't have to do the housework, Susanita", he tells me. "That's what Jomey's for." He goes on to tell me that my job is just to look beautiful, do my nails and things like that. "Let's go and have lunch at the steakhouse near the air base," he entices.

When we get back, Pedro is at least two sheets to the wind after drinking most of the bottle of red wine, has a slip-up when we make love, and climaxes! But I don't. In fact, I don't even get warmed up. I start mulling over what he says about looking beautiful. How boring is that? And doing my nails? I've never been very interested in my nails. In fact, I've never thought about them much at all except for the fact that mine always seem to accumulate dirt. Nails are just there, holding my fingers together.

Woe is me!

*The other girls at the boarding school have nicknamed me Surfie. I can't believe I'm here. I should have kicked up more of a stink—but I had no idea that that Mum and Dad would carry through on their plan and it would be **this** bad. It's like being in prison. But Mum and Dad had insisted. They said they were worried about me not passing the Intermediate and didn't like some of the new friends I was hanging around with.*

I hate sleeping in a dormitory, getting up at the crack of dawn in the cold and dark, three-minute showers, having to queue for the toilet, doing homework every night, fingernails in the apple pie, eating baked beans and peanut butter, going to chapel twice every day and church twice on Sundays, not having anyone decent to play tennis with, wearing uniforms even in our free time and, in particular, bloomers. I am so very unhappy.

In chapel, the headmistress asks everyone who's been in bed with another girl to stand up. God is watching, she says. More than half the school stands up.

Chapter 46

UN DESASTRE DESPUES DE OTRO

It's the beginning of June '72. Summer has finally decided to put in an appearance. It is a perfect sunny, windless Madrid day. But the warmer weather has made coaching a hard slog, and by the time I get home from work I am exhausted. I'll be glad when my contract is up. Saturdays are always the busiest. I have been on the court from early in the morning until late in the afternoon with beginners, my pet aversion. The one consolation is that at least Spanish children are well behaved. I don't have to exert a lot of extra energy keeping them in check. Nor do I have to duck balls with kids trying to brand me as they do in Australia. Some of the young senoritas even curtsy before they hold their racquets up in front of them in the ready position, watched avidly by their parents. Still, I've had it by the time I get home and am dying for a cup of tea. I put the kettle on, dumping my tennis bag and racquets on the bed on the run through.

When I come back into the bedroom after showering, most of my things are gone and Pedro is striding up and down the bedroom, ranting and raving. From the gist of things, it seems I've violated the sanctity of the matrimonial bed by leaving my sweaty tennis stuff on top of it. All I want to know is where's my bloody stuff? Pedro points towards the kitchen window. I race over and lean out. Sure enough, there is a small pile of my things scattered right beneath the window in the block next door. Pedro has already told me the block belongs to the Catholic Church. The whole space is enclosed by a high fence, with three rows of barbed wire on top and a padlocked gate. There is no way I am ever going to be able to get my things back.

"Bloody hell, Pedro," I yell, as I stomp out of the room.

But I can't stay mad at him for long, especially when he puts on my favourite record of Carlos Gardell, the Argentinian tango singer who is currently undergoing a revival in Madrid. He takes me in his arms. We start to dance. At the ballroom dancing classes at the Masonic Hall in Collaroy we only learnt the Barn Dance, the Pride of Erin, the Canadian Three Step and the Gypsy Tap. I've never danced the tango before. But Pedro is such a wonderful dancer, with the ability to lead masterfully as we glide up and down the room. All the while, Gardell throbs out his most popular song, about how he wants to die slowly, cutting his veins and letting his blood drip out drop by drop; how he can't stand living anymore without his love. The only way out for him is death. It's magic!

At least Pedro had the sense not to chuck my racquets out too. That would have been a major inconvenience I wouldn't like to even think about. I'm beginning to think that maybe Mum had a point about marrying someone from the same background and having things in common. I always thought her advice sounded so boring. Now I am beginning to think she is probably right. But I do love the tango.

A few days later, I am lying on the bed reading *The Women of Rome* when I hear the front door slam, announcing that Pedro is home from the stock exchange. The book I have my nose in is a pretty ordinary read. It is almost impossible to get anything decent in English in Madrid, due to censorship. Sometimes I get so desperate I even resort to reading an English magazine called *Woman's Own,* which gives housekeeping, cooking and childcare tips, or worse still *Hola,* the Spanish gossip rag, which is really scraping the barrel. When Pedro picks up the book and glances at the page I am reading, somehow the word "prostitute" jumps right off the page at him. He immediately does a complete wobbly, waves the book in the air, strides up and down the room, all the while shouting, "If you read books about these kind of disgusting things, the next minute you will turn into a prostitute."

I can't imagine how he could have possibly come up with this theory but it is certainly a giant leap of the imagination and, if you ask me, bloody ridiculous. I am finding sex is boring even with someone as gorgeous looking as Pedro. I certainly couldn't imagine doing it for a living with every Tom, Dick and Harry. Pedro grabs my book, strides into the kitchen, flings open the window and chucks it into the vacant block next door. I race over to the kitchen window and look out. It has landed right next to my tennis bag, which by now is looking very much the worse for wear.

I am in a complete dilemma. I don't know what to do. Is this normal behaviour for Spanish husbands?

Out on parole

Mum picks me up at Central Station. It's the June long weekend and I am home from boarding school. As usual, John and I are playing in a tournament. This one is in Bathurst.

We're staying in an old hotel with saggy beds, a share bathroom at the end of a lino hallway, and big country breakfasts. It rains on and off all weekend. We don't finish playing the finals until well after midnight on Monday. Laden down with our winnings of Corning ware and Waterford crystal glasses, Mum drives us back to Sydney through the fog while we all sleep soundly on the back seat.

Chapter 47

QUE DESASTRE ES ESO?

I haven't dared to tackle any other housework since the kitchen cupboards debacle but I am bored stiff, stuck at home except for the coaching. I certainly didn't have any idea how restrictive life was going to be now I am a senora. Except for work, I can't go out without Pedro. Being cooped up inside the apartment for long stretches is driving me nuts! Thank God for Henrietta. In order to relieve the boredom, I decide I'll give the ironing a go. I've ironed the odd thing in the past and don't think I'm too bad at it. In fact, it is probably the housekeeping skill I most prefer and am best at. Pedro normally takes all his shirts to the *lavenderia* down the road to be washed, and then Jomey irons them. I've noticed that there is a pile of about ten ready to go. I think I can knock them over in no time.

The reality is somewhat different. I haven't taken into consideration that I've never ironed a man's business shirt before. It turns out to be a tedious business involving quite a complex procedure. The first one takes me forever. I find it almost impossible to maintain my concentration. It is every bit as boring as cleaning the kitchen. I keep drifting off into la-la land and end up having to re-iron the sleeves several times. I find that when I iron one side, the other side creases up. And as for all the tiny pleats on the cuffs, they are impossible. By the third shirt, I am just about going round the bend. I decide to take a break and go for a walk around the neighbourhood.

When I come back, Pedro is home and in the process of examining the cuffs of one of his shirts. He is on fire! He proceeds to show me the ironed cuff.

"*Mujer, que disastro es eso?*" (What kind of disaster is this?)

Apparently I've crushed the pleats on the cuffs, an unforgiveable sin.

"You can't possibly expect me to wear a shirt like this!"

Oh dear! My career as a housewife is not getting off to a very good start. I burst into tears and lock myself in the bathroom.

The Tildesley Shield

It's hard work but I finally manage to persuade my parents to let me return to Sydney to finish my schooling. But I've decided that it's school, full stop, I don't like. I want to be either outside or dreaming. But here at SCEGGS Redlands even phys ed is held inside in the gym. There's no time for dreams in the school curriculum nor time to play tennis either. However, I win the Tildesley Tennis Shield, an annual tennis tournament held between all the girls' independent schools in NSW, wearing one of Mum's tennis dresses. Mine are way too short, according to the gym mistress. The teachers smile at me now. I suppose they think at least I'm good at something.

Chapter 48

VAYA QUE SORPRESA!

I am standing at the kitchen sink gazing out the window when I see a group of men with cameras opening the gate at the far end of the block of land next door. The Catholic Church must have given them permission to use the vacant block, which are in short supply in Madrid, except for the small public courtyards sandwiched between the blocks of flats where mothers take their children to play. They fight their way through the undergrowth until they come almost in line with my kitchen window. They look like some kind of film crew. They start setting up their equipment.

When one of the men wanders over near to our building and starts to pick up the various things that Pedro has chucked out of the window over the last couple of weeks, I quickly duck down below the level of the window so he can't see me. I can hardly stop myself from bursting in to fit of giggles as he unzips my tennis bag that I left so irreverently on the marital bed, then drops it like a hot potato because it is full of dirty tennis clothes which must really pong by now. He kicks at the book, "The Women of Rome" which I can see looks rather the worst for wear, then looks up at our building with a bewildered expression on his face. He is obviously trying to work out where these items have come from, because he then looks up at the sky. That's it. I can't take any more. I shimmy along the kitchen floor on my tummy. When I make it to the vestibule, I just roll around on the floor laughing until my jaws ache and my sides feel like they are surely going to split.

The Canopus Room, Pacific Hotel
MANLY

"You can't come in. You're under age," the bouncers manning the front door at the Can tell me. "No I'm not," I bluff. One of them shows me a newspaper cutting. "Fifteen," he says, pointing with his finger. I'm sprung. There I am, in a photo with footie player Bob Fulton at McDowells Department Store in Dee Why, receiving their annual Sports Award of the Year.

Chapter 49

DONDE ESTA HENRIETTA?

The following day, I can't find my beloved cat Henrietta. She's gone missing. I look for her everywhere around the apartment, and am starting to get quite desperate. She doesn't usually hide herself away. In fact, she generally prefers to sit in the gangway, so I can stroke her as I go past. I hope she hasn't snuck out the door, when Pedro left for the stock exchange.

By the time Pedro gets home I am close to tears. When I ask if he's seen Henrietta, he tells me he's given her away to Jomey. I am devastated. I really love my little cat. She does have a mind of her own and at times can be downright stubborn, but she's been such a good little friend to me. I try unsuccessfully to choke back my tears, but they cascade down my face.

"Henrietta is my cat," I sob. "You've no bloody right to give her away."

Pedro finally confesses that he doesn't like cats and in particular, Henrietta. Earlier in the day he'd caught her with her paw in his fish bowl. The previous afternoon, he'd found her sleeping on the bed on *his* side on *his* pillow. Anyway, he continues, she will be better off at Jomey's place because she lives in a ground floor flat with its own garden and she's been wanting a cat to catch mice.

I am furious. I stomp off to the bedroom, slamming the door hard behind me. I haul my old suitcase down from the top of the wardrobe and start packing. When he comes into the bedroom to see what I am doing, I tell him I can't take anymore. I'm leaving.

Pedro watches me silently, a tear inching its way down his face. He begs me not to go. He looks beseechingly through his tear-drenched lashes while he tells me how much he loves me. What can I do? He is just irresistible when he is like this. I unpack my suitcase and put all my stuff back into the wardrobe. A passionate make-up session ensues during which Pedro has another slip-up and climaxes (and I don't—in fact I don't even know what a climax feels like yet). Then we set off down the street to my favourite tapas bar. Garlic prawns, fresh crunchy bread and red wine always make me feel better.

When I come home from work the next day I am very surprised to find there is a dog on the balcony. It is quite big, although I can see that it is only a puppy. It still has that soft, gooey look in its eyes. Nothing bad has happened to it yet.

"He is a Norwegian hound," Pedro tells me proudly. "And he has an excellent pedigree. His name is Goz Zimetry."

He looks like one of those huskies pulling the sleds I used to see on *Sergeant Preston of the Yukon*, that old television programme about the Canadian Mounties.

It doesn't take long for Pedro to realise he's made a mistake, a big one. Maybe an apartment is not the best place for a large, active puppy. When we arrive home from the movies one afternoon later in the week, the balcony looks like a disaster area. Most of the soil which had been in the big pots is now intermingled with chewed-off pieces of plants, and is strewn all over the balcony. Goz has completely demolished all of Pedro's much prized pot plants. He is in big trouble. Pedro is distraught, to say the least—first his fish, now his beloved plants. For safety's sake, I decide to remove Goz from the scene of the crime and take him for a walk around the block, before Pedro contemplates taking any revenge.

Stuck out in the sticks

Slazenger's sends me in a team to play in a tournament at Garlagembone. It is a tiny village with only a post office, a couple of shops, the hotel and a few battered timber houses situated on the central western plains on the banks of the Castlereagh River. At night the captain of the team and the boys go out for a drink. I can't go, I'm too young. There's no television or radio—there's just nothing to do except get up to mischief. I short sheet the boys' beds, put their mattresses in the wardrobe and turn them back to the wall then tie their pyjama cords in knots. They are as drunk as skunks when they make their way upstairs to bed. All hell breaks loose when they discover their mattresses have disappeared, their sheets are in a tangle and they can't get into their pyjamas.

Next morning we are in big trouble. The manager asks us to leave. Fortunately the Captain manages to negotiate a reprieve by telling him that I have to play in the final.. I beat Jan Boyd.

Chapter 50

LAS LLAVES PERDIDAS Y OTRAS COSAS

The next morning Pedro is still hot under the collar about Goz's mischievous behaviour, as well as mourning the loss of his plants. As soon as he leaves for the stock exchange, I decide to take Goz for a ride in the country and let him have a good run around. It isn't a good life for an active puppy to be stuck in an apartment. I find it decidedly claustrophobic myself. Hopefully he'll sow all his wild oats while we are out so when he comes home, he won't get into any more trouble. I have my fingers crossed.

Madrid isn't at all like Sydney. One minute I am driving in between high-rise blocks, but once past the Plaza de Castilla, they stop abruptly. The next moment I am driving along in open country. There are no straggling outer suburbs with ever-increasing land sizes outside Madrid. Goz is in dog heaven. He loves going out in the car. He hangs his head out the window, with his mouth wide open, his tongue lolling out, almost appearing to be tasting freedom. We drive for a good half hour, passing where I'd visited Bob Barnete, before pulling over next to a large stretch of paddock with some nice shady trees. We slide under the fence, Goz bounding ahead. I repair under a large tree with my *Women's Own*, leaving Goz to explore.

Before too long I fall into a deep sleep and only wake when Goz starts licking my face. When I look at my watch I nearly have a fit. We are in big trouble. I am not going to be back in time to prepare lunch. Pedro is not going to be happy. Meals are like a religious experience for him. He savours each mouthful of food, reveres each sip of wine, and absolutely insists lunch is served punctually, right on the knocker at a quarter to three. To compound the situation, when I look around I can't find the car keys. Goz can be very playful and loves to abscond with things. He is also inclined to eat anything and everything he comes across. I look him dead in the eye to see if I can detect a guilty conscience, but he just gazes back at me innocently, wagging his tail.

I search all over for the keys, without success. I am almost crying tears of desperation. In the end I approach some men working on the railway track on the other side of the field, who are only too pleased to come to my rescue. It is not every day they get interrupted by *una extranjera muy guapa* (a pretty foreign girl) in such dire distress. They somehow manage to get the soft-top roof open without incurring too much damage and get the car started without the keys. I put the foot down, making it back home to Madrid in record time. Pedro is not impressed. But fortunately for me he's had a very good morning at the stock exchange, and suggests we go out for lunch.

Spaniards eat out a lot. Fortunately, there are lots of restaurants and they're not that expensive. It's not the custom in Spain to invite people to your home, except for family.

Our home back in Australia was busy, like Pitt Street everyone used to say. There were always lots of people coming and going all the time. Overseas, country and interstate players billeted with us when city tournaments were on. A few promising young boys from New Zealand even lived with us for several years. As long as they took their sandshoes off at the door, Mum didn't mind. Her theory was she'd much rather have us under her feet and know where we were. However, having to vacuum up ingrained loam out of the carpet from inconsiderate tennis players would have driven her nuts.

It takes a great deal of persuasion before Pedro eventually agrees that I can have a cocktail party and invite all my Australian friends from the embassy and some of the Episcopalians from the church in the Eurobuilding. I am beside myself with excitement when the great day arrives. I am eager to show off my handsome husband as well as the gorgeous new dress I've bought to wear for the occasion. The roof garden is the perfect venue.

I flit from person to person with gay abandon, chatting first with this one and then the next, totally oblivious of which sex they are. When I happen to look over at Pedro he is breathing fire but I am having such an interesting conversation with Andy, my friend Joyce's husband, that I can't drag myself away. He is regaling me with a story about one of the blokes from the Australian Embassy who he says is a terrible womaniser. When I turn around to check out the said fellow, I find it hard to believe because he is such an ordinary looking specimen and quite old.

"See his wife over there talking to that dark, attractive woman?" Andy continues.

I look over. "Yes."

"He has his eye on her now. But his wife always makes it her business to befriend any woman her husband sets his fancy on.

The prospective lovers always find that she is such a nice woman, that most potential affairs are nipped in the bud."

I look around again for Pedro, to discover that he is standing right behind me, talking to one of the girls from the embassy. I overhear him telling her how beautiful she is and declaring passionate love to her. However, I can see that he doesn't mean it, the way he is squeezing his eyes and glaring at me. I get the message. Gay social chit-chat is not in Pedro's repertoire. Once again I've obviously overstepped the mark and am most definitely in trouble. I am in no doubt that when everyone goes home it will be on for one and all.

And it is! Pedro rants and raves, waves his hands in the air while all the time striding back and forth. I don't know what to do. I have never heard Mum and Dad ever raise their voices at each other and only on the odd occasion with us. It had to be something really bad for that to happen. I have no idea how to handle this situation.

Now I'm in Whoop Whoop

This weekend we're playing in another country tournament—this one is at Barraba in New England on the Manilla River. I am staying with the Spencers on a farm just out of town. On the last night the boys I'm travelling with get absolutely plastered then go out pig shooting. They accidentally kill a sheep. We leave early the next morning before the word gets around. The boys are so hung over that they can hardly keep awake, let alone drive. I drive all the way in 4th gear because I don't know how to change gears.

Chapter 51

AHORA QUE SOY UNA SENORA

It is late afternoon. Pedro and I are walking up my favourite street in Madrid, the Avenida de Jose Antonio, on our way back from my Spanish and his English class at Berlitz. He is most annoyed. He says that I'm checking out the other men walking towards us. Perhaps I am, in between admiring the winged creatures on top of the buildings. The Spanish men are certainly very handsome. They are also extremely well turned out in their immaculate suits and so beautifully groomed, that this is probably the case. But if so, it is certainly without intent. And anyway, as Dad used to say, "You may as well put a deposit on a rosewood box when you stop looking." And I totally agree. I'll just have to be more surreptitious from now on.

I don't know what Pedro's worried about. Even with all our ups and down, there is no way I would be *interested* in anyone else. I can't understand how he can possibly be worried about where I look. Surely it is obvious that I am absolutely, totally, madly in love with him. Even though he *is* on the difficult side. *I* should be the one that is worried.

Every woman that passes by ogles him. Pedro always looks like he has just stepped out of a movie screen.

He turns on a hell of a tantrum when we get home, screaming, shouting, waving his arms, stamping, striding up and down. He finishes by telling me that now that I am a *senora,* I must keep my eyes looking downwards when I walk up the street. I'm beginning to wonder if it was a wise decision to marry in such haste. Things might have worked out better if we'd had more time to get to know each other. The truth of the matter is, with his current goings-on, I might not have made the same decision.

A few weeks later Pedro and I are invited by the First Secretary at the Australian Embassy to his apartment on the fourteenth floor overlooking the Castillano, to watch Franco's annual military parade. I am really looking forward to it. I've heard from other people at the embassy that this event is more of an excuse to get together for a jolly old time and a piss-up rather than an observance of Spanish military might. The tanks and artillery are purportedly relics from the Second World War and nothing to write home about. But what I am really looking forward to is speaking English and being with other Australians for a change. It'll be a bit of a rest from Pedro's intensity, which is akin to living on the side of a volcano.

At the last minute, when we are about to leave, Pedro decides that he doesn't want to go. This decision doesn't surprise me. He's been moping around all morning. He's not comfortable socialising at all really, but especially when everyone is speaking English and he can't understand what they are saying. He is certainly a bit put out when I say I am going anyway. I am all dressed up to the nines, and ready to go. There's no way I'm going to miss this get-together for quids although I'm disappointed that he won't come with me.

The old lift clanks its way up to the 14th floor of the First Secretary's apartment building with a great effort. When I finally get there, the door to the apartment is already open. In answer to my knock, the First Secretary's voice yells from the depths to come on in. I go down the hall and am somewhat taken aback to find everyone holed up in the bedroom. The First Secretary himself is in bed with one leg in plaster attached by a cord to the ceiling! As I stand outside the bedroom peering in, his wife comes up and whispers in my ear as she ushers me in, that he had a fall while going down to the cellar to get some beer at a recent party and has broken his leg.

There are about twenty people sitting and standing around the room, all well under way in the drinks department by the looks of things, while the First Secretary lies—face flushed, beer in hand, holding forth as usual. He is regaling the audience with blue jokes and laughing raucously. As the afternoon wears on, the party continues in this vein. We are all having such a good time that we completely forget to walk out on the balcony and watch the tanks go by. Intermittently, a few more stragglers drift in, red-faced and puffing. Apparently the lift has broken down and they've had to walk up the stairs, which doesn't surprise me at all. I felt it was on its last legs on the way up.

Suddenly, to my surprise, Pedro arrives!

"What is my wife doing in another man's bedroom?" he shouts.

Everyone thinks he is joking and laughs. I also find it hard not to laugh but try to stifle mine, because Pedro is definitely not laughing. In fact, his face is as black as thunder. He grabs me by the arm and insists that we leave immediately. Rather than create a scene, I pick up my bag and head for the front door, hoping that the other party-goers are so drunk they won't notice my sudden departure.

Pedro is furious with me when we get home for my lack of senora behaviour and can't understand how I could possibly agree to be in another man's bedroom. I, on the other hand, am totally pissed off with him for dragging me away from such a good party. "After all," I point out, "there were at least twenty other people in the bedroom."

We end up having another major argument, and then he leaves, disappearing into the night. I am so mad I start packing my bag again, but sit down on the bed in desperation. It is an empty threat really because I don't have enough money to go anywhere. I've spent the little I had left on clothes to make me feel better. Once again I do wish I had someone to discuss the situation with. I don't know what to do.

Me—an accountant????

I don't like working at G.M. Wayling Pty Ltd, Dad's accountants but Dad has always dreamed of having an accountant in the family. It is such a dreary, boring place. Every available surface is piled high with papers and files. I don't know how Mr Wayling can spend his life here. My job is to add up columns of figures then convert them into decimal currency. It never balances. Sometimes Mr Wayling gives me a letter to type. When he goes out to visit clients, I sneak into the doctor's reception area next door and nick some magazines. Sometimes I have a little snooze. Luckily the stairs creak so I can always hear him coming.

Chapter 52

LA VIDA DE UNA SENORA

My eating habits have completely changed. Those hearty Australian breakfasts of porridge, steak and eggs, numerous rounds of toast and marmalade washed down by cups of sweet, milky tea are now a thing of the past.

Breakfast is only a rumour here in Madrid. A cup of coffee and a piece of toast—and that's it! Then nothing until lunch, which is not until nearly three. I find that I am nearly falling over with starvation by then. I'm also used to having my main meal at night and feel quite cross making the changeover. But as the shops and businesses in Madrid close down between one and five, this is when people sit down to a three-course lunch usually washed down with wine. After lunch it is time for *la siesta*. Though generally speaking this is "frolic in the hay" time. Not a lot of *sleeping* is done! And there's certainly not a lot of work done *after* lunch, which Americans trying to do business here in Madrid find very frustrating.

Most weekday mornings, Pedro, dressed immaculately, heads off for the stock exchange. When Jomey arrives shortly afterwards to do the housework, if I'm not coaching, I head off to the Chamartin markets to buy food for lunch. If I hurry there and back, Jomey does all the cutting up for me before she leaves.

Pedro accompanied me to the markets the first time, to introduce me to his preferred stallholders and give me the drum on what to buy. I can't really go too far wrong because, although I've never done any food shopping before to speak of, Pedro told me that these markets are where all the bests chefs in Madrid shop and everything here is of the highest standard and very fresh. The stallholders also know that Pedro doesn't tolerate any poor quality food and will let them know in no uncertain terms, if something isn't up to scratch.

When I arrive early this particular morning the markets are already a hive of activity. It is certainly a very different shopping experience from Woolies at Narrabeen. The Chamartin markets comprise two enormous floors crammed with every food item imaginable. Huge legs of Jamon de Serrano and long, thin net bags of garlic hang from large hooks attached to the wooden rafters. Chickens, with their feathers still on but necks wrung, and whole, skinned lambs, pigs, calves and rabbits, are on display outside the butchers' shops. Long trestle tables are packed with an endless variety of delicatessen delights. Luminously yellow bananas swing from the top of the greengrocers' stalls. Trays are stacked high with a huge array of brilliantly coloured fruit and vegetables, and refrigerated cabinets display a multitude of cheeses, salchichas and chorizos. There is even a small café bar where I buy a *café con leche* and sip it slowly while I contemplate what I am going to serve for lunch.

My repertoire is still somewhat limited but after careful consideration I decide to make the baked fish dish with 23 cloves of garlic that Pedro has shown me how to cook.

It is pretty foolproof. I'll serve it with salad and some fresh crunchy bread.. Pedro still has to take it easy with his diet so I don't have to worry about dessert.

I make it back in time for Jomey to peel all the garlic, thank goodness. She also helps me with the salad dressing before she goes home for the day, so I am running right on time. But by three o'clock Pedro hasn't shown up which is bloody annoying. I am becoming crosser by the minute. He is always so insistent that his lunch is ready right on time on the days I don't coach. An hour goes by and he still hasn't arrived. I am so angry that I tip the lot down the garbage disposal unit and press the button. The lunch is completely ruined anyway. The fish is way over-cooked and I've made the mistake of putting the dressing on the salad so it has gone soggy.

I feel down in the dumps after all that effort going to waste. Being a Spanish housewife is a thankless bloody task, worse than tennis coaching or secretarial work, I decide. Spanish men think they are the kings, and expect their wives to kowtow. I feel like I am being treated like a second-class citizen and don't like it. I decide to shoot through with Goz because when Pedro arrives home he will not be at all impressed with the "no lunch" situation.

Fortunately, I'm still out walking with Goz when Pedro gets home. He takes off down the road to one of the local restaurants and doesn't come back until late in the evening—still very miffed. I get the feeling that I'm supposed to be at his beck and call.

I'm definitely out of my depth

"Have you heard about the Collaroy Grunter?" a good-looking surfie with olive skin, blonde hair and blue eyes asks. "She grunts for the boys in the surf club. See that room at the back," he says, pointing to a door which is slightly ajar between the men's and ladies' toilets. "That's where it happens. The boys all queue up outside and wait their turn."

I never go back to Collaroy Beach.

Chapter 53

LA LIBERACION DE LAS MUJERES

Joyce, who I met at the First Secretary's party, calls to ask if I would mind taking an Australian girl around Madrid tomorrow because she has an appointment with her obstetrician. No probs, I tell her. She goes on to say that the girl is around my age. I couldn't care less how old she is. I am always desperate to speak English and would agree to meet almost anyone. And the fact that she is Australian is an additional bonus! I don't have any close friends here in Madrid. I've never been a person who has lots of girlfriends—usually just the one, and so far, I haven't really met anyone I've really clicked with. I find it difficult not having someone to confide in, especially in my current situation. I really like Joyce but she is a lot older than me, has two children, is an executive wife and is always very busy.

Annabel Hall is someone I would normally never meet. She is on the academic side, not at all sporty. She tells me that she has left her husband back in Sydney because she's decided that she doesn't want to be a wife anymore. She is a *feminist* and a member of *the Women's Liberation*

Movement, she tells me. I am living in a vacuum here in Madrid where everything is censored and very little news, decent books and magazines filter through. I haven't heard anything about feminists—nor for that matter, the Women's Liberation Movement. I am also absolutely positive that one of the last things Spanish men would want their wives to know about is women's liberation. They like to keep their women in their place at home and preferably, from what I've noticed, continuously pregnant. Spain is in a lot of ways at least 30 years behind the times in most things compared to Australia. Only recently I saw on the news that the coming of age for women in Spain has been reduced from 32 to 27. Mum told me in one of her recent letters that in Australia they are just considering lowering it from 21 to 18. And of course, in Spain there is no divorce!

I notice that Annabel doesn't wear a bra and wonder if this is part of feminism and the women's liberation, but don't dare ask. She is decidedly intimidating. We spend the day walking in the Club de Campo, the same park where Carlos and I spent our first date. Goz is beside himself, romping alongside, straining on the lead in all directions. In the afternoon when we hire a row boat, he sits up the front, leaning forward with his tongue out, loving every minute of it.

When Annabel starts talking, I realise that I haven't heard any news from back home to speak of at all really. Mum's letters tend to be about the various doings of family and friends, interspersed with some local tennis gossip. But Annabel is certainly all fired up about feminism and women's lib. She tells me that she just can't understand how I put up with Pedro.

"From what I've heard from Joyce, he's a real male chauvinist pig," she says.

She continues in this vein, really trying to stir me up with a certain degree of success. I've never really thought about this kind of thing much before. I always just assumed that I would follow in Mum's footsteps. Once I married and had a family, I would stay at home. In my opinion Mum has a good life—playing tennis three days a week, going for a swim if it is a hot day, and doing all kinds of other hobbies and things she likes. The only inconvenience is that she has to do the shopping, cooking and housework. However, she always seemed to have things under control and still has plenty of time to enjoy herself. I've certainly found most of the work I have done to date, especially office work and tennis coaching, nothing to get excited about. In fact, they are downright boring. I would be only too glad to give them the flick.

Still, I am finding life as a Spanish housewife dull and very restrictive. I can't just come and go as I am used to, except for going to work and trips to the supermarket. (Even then, one day, I saw Pedro creeping along the next aisle, keeping an eye on me to ensure that I didn't run off with one of the other customers or perhaps the checkout boys who must be all of ten years old.) If I want to go to the tennis club or the movies, I can't go by myself. Spanish convention dictates that unless my mother or some other suitable older "female" accompanies me, I have to wait and go with Pedro. Otherwise all hell will break loose and it just wouldn't be worth the effort.

I'm so very cross!

I've always wanted to work in a shop. Although Dad has given up his plan for me to be an accountant, he now thinks I should be a secretary. If I'm on my feet all day, I'll get varicose veins, he says. Then no one will want to marry me. Dad gets me a job with Uncle Alf at his pharmacy in North Narrabeen. For three days, I dust the shelves. I haven't been near a customer or the cash register. Finally, I'm sent to pick up some merchandise in Narraweena. It is boxes of Modess sanitary napkins—very clearly labelled and displayed in my car window as I drive back. I am humiliated. Everyone I know, and even some I don't, toot me. I'm in tears as I walk up the driveway at lunchtime. My brother starts laughing! "Dad told Uncle Alf to make sure you don't like shop work." I am furious. I go into my bedroom and pack my suitcase. I put it outside my door. It's full of shoes because I can't decide what else to take.

Chapter 54

LA LUNA DE MIEL

We haven't been on our honeymoon yet. We've had to put it on hold until I worked out my six-month coaching contract with the Castillian Tennis Association. However, even though we've now been married for a couple of months I am decidedly nervous about going away and being with Pedro full time. I'm still not used to living with him, and never know what kind of mood I am going to find him in or what he is going to do next. Although back home in Australia, our family has had its moments as most families do, I've decided that we are a pretty easy-going lot on the whole. Pedro, on the other hand, is most definitely not. If things aren't just perfectly in accordance with his own very particular criteria—kerboom!!!!

One of the things which really sets Pedro off is dust. Not a skerrick of dust dares show its face in our apartment if it values its life. However, keeping surfaces dust free is easier said than done—much easier. Madrid is the third most polluted city in the world and as fast as you remove the fine dust, which settles on every available surface and in every nook and cranny, it reappears. Pedro is fanatical about ousting it and pursues its removal with a vengeance. He insists that Jomey wipes over every single item of furniture then vacuums and mops right through the apartment every day. This includes moving all the furniture, including the bed, and vacuuming under it as well. It's the type of detailed cleaning people do in Australia when they put their houses up for sale. Pedro also insists on clean sheets every day! I have to admit climbing into fresh-smelling sheets is quite delicious, but definitely, in my humble opinion over the top. He is also just as fastidious personally and spends what seems like forever in the bathroom with the door locked, primping. But he certainly does an excellent job because when he comes out he always looks exceptional.

Finally, I complete my contractual obligations with the Castillian Tennis Association and we are free to leave on our honeymoon. On the first day, we drive out of Madrid mid-morning and head north towards the Basque country. Pedro tells me as we drive along that we are going to Biarritz, and that we'll probably stay overnight on the way. There is a restaurant he wants to take me to. I'm not sure where Biarritz is and as I don't want to show my ignorance, I just smile. Smiling isn't an easy thing to do by any means because I'm prone to carsickness and am already feeling a bit queasy. Pedro is driving like a maniac as usual, which doesn't help matters. When I steal a quick look at the speedo, it shows that we are going over 165 kilometres an hour. To make matters worse, he is also smoking his stinky big cigars one after another with the windows up and the air-conditioning on.

We arrive for a late lunch at Les Panniers, a large old barn of a place situated at the base of gently rolling hills, surrounded by billiard lawns. Pedro has already told me that it is a favourite spot for Basque weddings. As we step inside, I am confronted by the most amazing spectacle. The restaurant is packed to the rafters. Downstairs, an exuberant crowd is attending a wedding. Huge trestle tables are loaded down with enormous quantities of food and bottles of wine. The bride and groom, who are both on the hefty side, are tucking in as though they haven't eaten all week. So are several priests who are also seated at the main table. We sit upstairs, which is also full, overlooking all the activity. It is better than going to the theatre. I am so engrossed in watching all the goings-on that I can hardly concentrate on the menu. Pedro advises me that the tapas are the specialty of the house and promises me that I won't need a second course. But as usual, I am starving and my eyes are way bigger than my stomach. Plus, one of my favourite dishes, garlic chicken, is on the menu. I insist on ordering it.

When the tapas start arriving one after another, I begin to think that perhaps I've made a mistake. By the fifteenth plate, my stomach starts to ache and I am beginning to feel slightly queasy. When I ask Pedro how many plates altogether, he tells me 32. He should have told me beforehand. Even someone like me, whose eyes are *always* bigger than their stomach, would *surely* have gotten the message. Unfortunately, it is too late to cancel my order. I can't even bear looking at the garlic chicken when it arrives, let alone eating it. I avert my eyes and don't manage even the smallest piece.

Biarritz is in the Basque country in France and I am ecstatic when we arrive because it has a surf beach. I didn't realise how much I've been missing the smell of salt air. We find a small pensione to stay in, only a few minutes' walk from the beach.

When I awake the next morning, I can hear one of my favourite sounds—waves crashing onto the sand. In the afternoon, as Pedro and I wander along the edge of the water, the waves lap over my feet and although it is still too cold for a swim, I am in heaven. Before dinner that night, we play ten pin bowls and although it is a tight game, Pedro wins. The win, combined with a delicious bottle of Rioja with dinner, puts him in an excellent frame of mind, causing him to completely forget about "not climaxing". Maybe this time I'll get pregnant.

It's a numbers game

Two is a kiss, four is upstairs outside, six downstairs inside, eight downstairs outside, 10 downstairs inside, 12 is a dry root and 14 is going all the way. I go out with six different guys in a row. They all put the hard word on. As soon as they stop the car at the end of an evening out, they pounce. In desperation, I ask Mum what I should do. It is not a pleasant experience being rugby tackled in the car on the way home. I dread the last part of the evening because I know what's coming up. Some of the boys even take the door handle on the passenger side off so I have to quickly wind the window down and reach out to open the door. Another boy leaves me at the top of Long Reef when I won't come good! I have to walk home in the dark. When I ask Mum what to do she warns me that men won't marry used goods.

Chapter 55

RAMONA LA MADRE DE PEDRO

I am feeling very anxious, because today I am going to meet my mother-in-law for the first time. I often wondered why nobody from Pedro's family came to our wedding but I put this down to the fact that it was such a rushed affair. I would have liked my family to be there too but that would have delayed things for ages.

Pedro has told me a few things about his mother already. For one thing, she won't get into a car. She says they go so fast they make her dizzy. I'm not surprised if she's been in the car with Pedro, especially if he was smoking one of those dreadful cigars. That's enough to make anyone dizzy. But she doesn't like planes either and is always sending newspaper cuttings to Pedro of every aeroplane crash and near-miss from around the world. Needless to say, he is *paranoid* about plane travel and avoids it at all costs. And although he has assured me that his family aren't religious, I just hope his mother won't have it in for me because I'm not a Catholic.

When we arrive at Bilbao, we go straight to the factory that Pedro owns (it's the first I've heard of it), where they manufacture chorizos and salchichas for the *charcuteria* (delicatessen) that his sisters run in town. It is just after lunch. As we come in the door, I notice a man leaning on the wall, fast asleep. I have never seen anything so funny! He is even snoring. It reminds me of when Terese and I travelled from Oviedo to Madrid, packed like sardines in third class, and slept standing up. But this bloke doesn't even need propping up. He certainly must have been doing a fair bit of practice to be able to maintain his balance like he does. Pedro, however, doesn't think it is funny at all. The bloke turns out to be Luiz, Pedro's brother-in-law, who is the factory manager and in charge of operations.

Pedro does his loll completely! He gives his brother-in-law the rounds of the kitchen and definitely doesn't mince his words. I feel shattered just listening to it.

The next day, when we go for lunch with Pedro's family, his mother doesn't join us. She takes one look at me then scurries into her bedroom, turns the light off and refuses to come out. I certainly don't seem to have much luck with Spanish mothers.

The lunch is enormous. There are four courses—soup, fish, chicken then meat, with lots of bread and red wine, and brandy afterwards. No wonder poor Luiz fell asleep after eating. I can hardly keep awake myself. But I force myself to because this afternoon I am going to help Luz and Esperanza, Pedro's sisters, in their charcuteria. I can hardly wait! Shop was my favourite game as a child and now I am going to get to do it for real.

Pedro's mother remains holed up in the bedroom with the lights out, despite Pedro's many entreaties, as well as threats to call the doctor. It is beginning to get me down. She must come out when I'm not there. She has to. There's no toilet.

Working in the charcuteria is such fun. I love serving the customers. Although at the start I find it a bit tricky, because the Spanish women like to buy very small quantities of everything and are very exact about how much they want, only 100 grams of this and 150 grams of that, not a skerrick over and all sliced paper thin. But by the end of the afternoon I am getting the hang of it and having a ball.

The following day we leave for the family's holiday flat on the beach. Pedro has already warned me that it is basic, but that's okay with me. I am really looking forward to walking up and down the beach, and as the weather has warmed up considerably over the last couple of days, I'll probably be able to take a dip. One thing is for sure, I'll be pleased to get away from Pedro's mother. I've hardly set eyes on her the whole time we've been here but her presence hovers ominously over me whenever I'm in the apartment. When I ask Pedro why she is behaving like she is, he brushes it off.

Basic is not the word to describe the family holiday flat. I don't know where the builder who constructed these apartments got his licence or if he could possibly have one. It is hard to believe that the block of flats is only a few years old. The outside walls are already cracked, crumbling and water stained. On entering the main vestibule, it feels damp and I can smell sewerage. The apartment itself is also a shocker, in particular the kitchen, which looks like I've put it together. The cupboards are all higgledy-piggledy, with none of the doors able to be shut properly, and the counter top is so low that I have to kneel down to use it. As for the sink, it hasn't been put in straight and has sunk particularly badly at one end. The parquet floor has also been poorly laid and is already lifting in quite a few places. As for the lift, I downright refuse to go up and down in it because if the builder has had anything to do with it, it is bound to get stuck.

I was really looking forward to going to the beach. But when I take my clothes off to lie down on my towel, Pedro nearly has a fit and wants me to cover up immediately even though I am wearing a most respectable one-piece costume, not one of my teeny-weeny Australian bikinis! Then he would really have something to carry on about. He insists that I walk down to the water with my towel wrapped around me, only taking it off at the very last minute before I get into the water. Pedro refuses to get into the water himself. He just hangs around down at the edge on guard duty with my towel, ready for when I get out, glaring at anyone who dares come near.

After the beach, we go shopping. I try on the most gorgeous, sexy yellow outfit. But Pedro wants me to get a matronly looking navy blue suit and storms out of the shop when I won't agree with him. We make up over dinner when he prepares my favourite Basque dish, *baccalao* in tomato sauce, which we wash down with a bottle of dark rich red Vino de Pomal. As I lick the last of the sauce off my fingers and sip the last drop of wine in my glass, he tells me how beautiful I am and how much he loves me. "Jekyll and Hyde," I decide. Pedro is certainly difficult, has some bad points and is moody but he can also be very charming. He certainly is a magnificent cook. I really love good food.

After a week at the holiday flat we return to Bilbao for another couple of days. As his mother is still absolutely refusing to come out of her bedroom, I am very pleased when Pedro decides that we'll head off for Asturias.

We stop for lunch at Santurce, a small port an hour out of Bilbao, where all kinds of old fishing boats in the harbour are unloading the previous night's catch. White-aproned men are cooking small fish on barbecues around the wharf area.

"*Sardinas*," Pedro tells me.

But they don't look at all like the sardines we get at home in those roll-top tins. Nor do they taste like them. When I put one in my mouth, it is delicious. It has been cooked so it is very crispy. I eat the whole fish —the head, including the eyes, although I do spit the eyeballs out, plus the tail and all the bones. I can't imagine what they would think back home about this little effort.

In the evening we eat at a small outside restaurant beside a river, with old trestle tables and benches made of roughly hewn wood. The smell of fresh bread wafts through the air from an old brick oven. There are fish frying on a large hot plate over a barbecue and an old man is picking fresh salad leaves from a garden at the rear of the building. The food is scrumptious.

As we munch on the bread and salad, a younger man trudges by with a bucket full of freshly caught fish. The sun goes down behind the hills and an old tabby cat wanders up, then waits hopefully at my feet. I realise there is nothing to compare to eating like this. It is a sublime experience and I will be very lucky to fit into any of my clothes if I keep on eating so much every day. I've already had trouble getting my zipper up!

The following morning, we make love. Is that what it is? It is really starting to get to me. To make matters worse, Pedro has his mind on the job today and doesn't climax so there is not even the possible consolation of falling pregnant. I wonder whether I will have to spend the rest of my life "girding my loins and thinking of the Queen" like I'd once overheard Mum tell a friend that it was a woman's duty to do?

Later that day we eat lunch in Isla, a seaside village with craggy cliff faces, battered rocks jutting out of the water and sandy beaches. We sit at a table on the beach while lobsters are fished out of a large pool for our lunch. I have to turn my head and not look at the poor creatures, because although I do like fresh seafood, this is a bit too close to home. So I sip some wine and stare into Pedro's eyes to take my mind of things. How good looking can a bloke be? His skin is perfect, almost luminous. Not a mark on it. I bet he's never had a pimple in his life. His teeth are also perfect and gleam in the midday sun. He's already told me that he's never had a filling. Maybe the fact that he looks so good is why he is so difficult to get on with. He's probably never had to make an effort. Not like me. I had to work hard, especially in the teenage pimples/braces-on-the-teeth period. I can remember times when I felt moody, especially at a bad time of the month, and Mum always told me to pull up my socks because no-one would like me if I wasn't nice.

When the lobsters arrive they are served steaming hot and delicious. We eat them with our fingers then suck them dry.

The drive through Asturias is stunningly beautiful. As we move away from the coast we pass through gently rolling hills then into a land of high snow-capped mountains. The Picos de Europa, Pedro tells me, which tower over fast flowing rivers, vast orchards and tiny farmhouses. In the early evening, we arrive at Leon where Pedro lived at one time when he was young. We park in the centre of town where we chance upon some old friends of his outside the cellar door of their wine shop. They insist that we come in and try some of their wines and freshly made chorizos, hot out of the pot. What heaven, but I can feel my stomach expanding even more. I don't know how we manage it, but after consuming several chorizos and a couple of glasses of red, we back up for another huge meal in a beautiful old restaurant nearby.

Afterwards we go for a stroll to the main plaza then around the beautiful old Leon cathedral, Catedral de Santa Maria. As we approach it is dark except for the light which shines through the stained-glass windows. Lacy stone spires spear into the darkness and a statue of St James on horseback appears to be galloping down one side of the building—certainly a bit different to St Faiths, the square red brick church of my childhood.

The following day we go to Pedro's village, Veneros, the one he'd told me about over our first lunch. We drive to Bonar, a small village outside of Leon, and park the car at the back of the house of one of Pedro's cousins. It is then that I discover there is still no road to Veneros and we'll have to walk more than twenty kilometres each way. It turns out not to be an easy walk by any means. It is still only a narrow mountainous and very stoney track, which wends its way up and down until it reaches the village. I trudge along, not at all happy as I am only wearing my well-worn Dunlop Volleys and the surface is very rough. I can feel every rock and stone through the thin soles and later, when I take my shoes off, I discover my feet are beginning to sprout blisters.

As I make my way dispiritedly up the main street of the small village, which is only a single-lane, uneven dirt road lined with about a dozen old houses on either side, I am in shock. It is so primitive. It's hard to imagine my debonair, always immaculately dressed husband living here. At the top end of the street, there is a swift-flowing stream where black-clad women have wedged themselves between rocks in three-pronged clogs to do their washing. There is still no running water inside the houses, or any electricity either. The only telephone in the village is in the small general store which at one time, Pedro divulges, his mother used to run.

Rising up behind the village is el Cerro Cogolla, which at this time of the year is covered in brightly coloured yellow and purple flowers. Pedro's face is shining with exhilaration. He is on his home turf and loving every moment. He is champing at the bit to take off up the mountain but I've had enough. We've still got to walk back to Bonar. I find this kind of exercise much harder than a game of tennis. I lie down on the grass and fall into the deepest sleep, vividly dreaming about me in three-pronged clogs clinging onto rocks, trying desperately to keep my balance in fast-flowing streams. The worry is that Pedro has told me he would like to live in Veneros one day, but in my wildest dreams I can't imagine living here. He can't possibly be serious!

Australian Hardcourt Championships
NAMBOUR, QUEENSLAND

NO. 1 JUNIOR SEED LOSES

Sixteen-year-old Sue Alexander, of Manly, caused an upset by beating the State's number one junior seed, Helen Goulay, in the Metrolpolitan Hardcourt Championships yesterday.

In a women's singles match at Naremburn, she won 9-7, 7-5.

I'm finding it difficult to concentrate on tennis because of this tall, good-looking, blonde bloke with green eyes. His name is Harry. I try to attract his attention by hanging around the court where he's playing, wearing my most daring outfit—shorts and a low halter top. I succeed. He invites me for a drive in his cool, pale blue MGB with a dark blue glass sun-roof. He's twenty-six and wants to have sex with me. It's easy for me to refuse. I don't have any sexual feelings. They are buried deep down inside me and that's where they are going to stay. I don't want to get hurt again. I tell him I'm sixteen and a virgin. He says I shouldn't dress like I do.

Chapter 56

UNA VISITA CON LEW Y JENNY HOAD

Halfway through our honeymoon, we drive back via Madrid, where we spend a few days checking up on the home front, and grabbing a quick change of clothes. It is going to be a lot warmer down south on the Costa del Sol at our next destination, Fuengirola, where we plan to visit Jenny and Lew Hoad at their Campo de Tenis.

On the way, we stop at Cordoba, one of my favourite Spanish cities. In the early evening, as we stroll hand in hand down Calleja de las Flores, the poignant magic of the husky-voiced gypsies belting out flamenco songs echoes from the white stucco tavernas lining the narrow street. Vibrantly coloured flowers peer out from the hanging wall pots on nearby balconies and poke their heads over the walls surrounding ancient Moorish courtyards.

We spend the next night in Granada and visit La Alhambra. In the late afternoon we clamber up cobbled, walled lanes to the top of the remains of the last Moorish stronghold, where we watch the brilliant rays of the setting sun transform the entire hill of La Sabica into gold.

I am bursting with excitement when we arrive at Jenny and Lew Hoads' tennis club in Fuengirola. It is so great to see Jenny, a fellow Pisces, again, and also to have some people around me who speak English. Some are even Australians! Sometimes I think I will go crazy in Madrid. The only English I've spoken recently is to the people from the embassy (but that is only every now and then, as Pedro seems to have taken an intense dislike to them after the First Secretary's party), and on Sundays, with the Episcopalians, after the service. But this can be a pretty boring line of chat, especially when they start dissecting the sermons or discussing Bible readings.

I am feeling a bit down because I am still not pregnant, despite several slip-ups by Pedro. It is all I can think about. Some kind of hormonal imbalance must have occurred in my body and invaded my mind because I've never thought of having a baby before. I hope I will get a chance to talk about it with Jenny.

Lew and Jenny's club is just as beautiful as I remember it from when I played the tournament here a couple of years earlier when Jenny and I slogged it out in a torrid three-hour match in the finals on a boiling hot day. I narrowly won 13–11 in the third. The dark red bougainvillea, which is climbing over the white stucco buildings and up the tennis court fences, is in full and radiant flower, as are the vibrantly pink lilies in the ponds between the courts. The little restaurant, which Jenny designed, is now finished. With its dark wooden tables and benches and rock walls, it is just like a Spanish taverna, except for the assortment of ancient tennis racquets and photos of Lew in his heyday.

Jenny and Lew are very surprised to find out that I am married, and even more so to a Spaniard. I was sure that Jenny, more than anyone, would understand my strong attraction to

Pedro, who is every bit as gorgeous as Lew and can be just as charming. I don't let on to them how quickly it all happened, as I am sure they'll think I must be pregnant too.

Pedro and I find a room in a little pensione in Mijas, a small pueblo of white stucco buildings nestled into the hillside overlooking the sea just up the hill from the tennis club. However, we spend most of our time at the club. Pedro insists that I play tennis with him every day. I've never been much good with beginners. I just don't have the patience and find it very boring, even if they are devastatingly handsome. Despite all the lessons Pedro has been having, he is still not much more than a beginner.

Jenny arranges for me to play a couple of games with some of the other guests who are better players. Unfortunately, I hurt my knee during a vigorous game of doubles with three Aussie blokes. When I go in to have some treatment with the resident French physio, Christian, Pedro goes off in a huff, marches out of the club and takes off in his car back to Mijas, leaving me to trudge back up the hill. I am furious. Each step I take is agony; my knee still hurts like hell, and to make matters worse, I have developed a splitting toothache.

When I arrive and explain my predicament to Senora Cortes, the old Spanish lady who owns the pensione, she tells me that there isn't a dentist for miles and gives me a small flask of vodka.

"Just swill it around the tooth," she tells me.

Yuk, vodka—not my favourite tipple. But believe it or not, it works although I do end up feeling rather dizzy, because some of the vodka ends up going down my throat. Blow me down if it doesn't fix my knee as well!

When I finally get back to our room, Pedro starts ranting and raving that I have been alone in a room with the door closed with "another man" and accuses me of having sex with the French physio. He's got to be joking. But once again he is deadly serious. Surely his behaviour can't be normal, even for a Spaniard!

Semi-finals Metropolitan Grasscourt Championships
LYONS ROAD, STRATHFIELD

The sun is beating down and I am sweating so profusely that the racquet keeps slipping around in my hand. I am well past my second wind and am unsure if I can last the distance. Evonne on the other hand looks cool, calm and collected at the other end of the court. It's 14 all—deuce. I've lost count of how many deuces we have played. I serve wide to Evonne's forehand. The ball skids through. My ad. The next rally goes on until I blast the ball deep into her backhand then move to the net. The ball whizzes past me, clipping deep on the side line. The crowd rises to its feet and applauds loudly. Deuce. Evonne walks to the net and talks to the umpire who then announces, "Miss Goolagong is unable to continue the match due to cramps. Game set match to Sue Alexander 6–3, 5–7 14 all."

Chapter 57

TODAVIA NO ESTOY
EMBARAZADA

Back in Madrid, I calculate that we've been married for over four months and I *still* haven't fallen pregnant. I am getting more desperate by the day to have a baby. It is all I can think about. But the way things are going, I just can't see how it is ever going to happen. The odds are stacked against me. Apart from a few slip-ups in the heat of the moment, usually after a good Rioja at dinner, Pedro is continuing with his very weird notions about sex. Unfortunately, I didn't manage to have a chat with Jenny while we were in Fuenjirola. Trying to keep a lid on all the uproar about the French physio, I didn't get a chance.

Pedro is not only absolutely convinced that he will lose his strength by climaxing, he also doesn't want to have sex too often for the same reason. Well I don't really mind about not having sex too often. It's certainly not all it is cracked up to be. When I press him on *exactly* how it would affect him he says that according to the ancient Chinese when a man ejaculates he loses "power" or vigour. He believes that every orgasm represents "energy suicide", a leakage of the body's innate strength. Male ejaculation is to be controlled as much as possible, otherwise a man is left vulnerable to disease, old age and general bad health, he advises.

I have Buckley's chance of getting pregnant at this rate.

I am also sure it isn't easy for Pedro to put the brakes on his sexuality because he's now started a heavy exercise programme. He insists on getting up at 5am when it is still dark and going out to the country for a fourteen-kilometre run. Unfortunately, he insists I join him on these excursions. Goz is the only one who is really happy about this turn of events, smiling exuberantly from ear to ear as he gallivants about. But I definitely don't like it. I'm used to sleeping in. Getting up so early makes me feel cranky for the rest of the day.

Now he has decided on a new tactic to try to take my mind off procreation for a while. He tells me that he isn't going to the stock exchange during the upcoming week. Instead he is going to take me for a few sightseeing trips around Madrid and nearby towns.

Our destination on the first day is the Sierra de Guadarrama, a mountain range about 50 kilometres out of Madrid where people go to ski in winter and hike in summer. Madrid is 650 metres above sea level and the weather is a bit like Canberra's, especially in the colder months when bitingly cold winds blow straight of the snowy mountains just like they do in our national capital.

Goz, of course, is beside himself because he is coming too. Although I love Madrid, it is somewhat of a relief to get out of the hustle and bustle and into open country and be able to breathe some fresh air for a change. Due to the pollution in Madrid, sometimes when I'm downtown, I feel quite dizzy from the lack of oxygen in the air. Factory emissions and the smoke and fumes emitted from the back of the old Seats due to the low-grade petrol are, I'm sure, the main culprits.

Pedro is being absolutely charming and for once eases back on the accelerator and gives those smelly cigars a breather. As we wend our way round hairpin bends, up slopes and through dense forests of pine, tawny vultures circle overhead looking for prey. It is hard to believe we are so close to Madrid. It feels like we are in another world completely. There is still some snow on the mountains and when we stop to take a break, Goz leaps out of the car and bounds gleefully away. His normal somewhat timid nature forgotten and his Norwegian genes coming to the fore, he skids down an ice patch, rolls over in the powdery snow and then tries to eat it. He races back up the hill then stands in front of us, wagging his tail in delight. He is in dog heaven.

We drive on to a local beauty spot, La Pedriza, a huge mass of smooth, sculpted granite, then hike nearby in complete silence among rock-roses, lavenders and heather. Ravenously hungry by lunchtime, we stop and eat a hearty roast at Alameda village then proceed to the Monastery El Escorial, the burial place of most of the Spanish monarchs since Phillip II. Afterwards we go to El Valle de los Caidos, a monument to the victims of the Spanish Civil War. We pass through the fantastic medieval village of Pedraza and historical Segovia on our way back to Madrid.

Pedro's strategy works. I don't think about babies all day. My mind is completely distracted, thinking what it would be like to have the experience of a civil war in your country. Over 500,000 people died in Spain during theirs and it only finished in 1939, which is not all that long ago comparatively. A lot of the men I coach who are now in their 50s would have been old enough to have lived through it—maybe even fought. Just recently I discovered that Generalissimo Franco was *still* issuing death warrants on his own deathbed in 1975 so it's no wonder people didn't discuss politics. I can't imagine anything like this ever happening in Australia—a political difference most likely would end in a bit of a biff followed up with a beer.

The following day we head for El Pardo, a small town on the outskirts of Madrid where Franco has lived since the end of the Civil War, in the Palacio Real del Pardo which had formerly been the summer residence of the Spanish kings until Alfonso XIII. The village of El Pardo is a quiet backwater and there aren't many people living here. Pedro tells me the population derives mainly from descendants of people in service at the Palacio Real del Pardo, the workers for the Patrimonio Nacional who administer the Royal Sites, and the Royal Guard.

"There is very little commerce in the town as you will see," he continues. "Only bars, restaurants and a few small businesses. And the retail area can't really be expanded because of the surrounding protected natural area of Monte del Pardo, which was once used as royal hunting grounds."

All the restaurants are renowned for their good food but Pedro, who always knows the best places to eat, selects La Choza de Segoviana which is housed in an 18th century building in the middle of a park and specialises in traditional local dishes. The *cocido* is the specialty and is served in three separate courses. However, today we are here for the rabbit, which Pedro says comes from the Pardo grounds. It is served in lots of garlicky tomato sauce and is absolutely delicious with more the texture of chicken, certainly a lot better than those tough, stringy bunnies sold by the "Rabbitoh" man back home that had to be stewed up for hours.

We wander hand in hand around our next destination, Toledo, which is about 70 kilometres out of Madrid. I love it. Toledo is full of wonderful, architecturally diverse old buildings built during the extensive period known as La Convivencia, when Jews, Christians and Muslims coexisted in harmony until King Ferdinand and Queen Isabella gave the Jews the flick in the late 1400s, unless they converted to Catholicism.

In the garrison of the Alcazar Pedro and I listen to muffled voices depicting the famous siege by the Republican forces in 1936. The Nationalist forces led by the Commandant of the Alcazar were besieged for 70 days. During this period, the Republicans captured and killed Commandant Moscardo's sixteen-year-old son. It was this event that steeled the Nationalist forces to their acceptance of starvation and death, because who could complain about what the siege was costing him, when the Commandant had given his son? Eventually Generalissimo Franco's forces advancing from the Extremadura were able to relieve the garrison.

Later we visit the Museo de Santa Cruz, housed in the old hospital, where we view many of El Greco's haunting paintings. We eat a light lunch of *bocadillo de manchego* and an *ensalata Russa* (Pedro just can't resist anything Russian) in an alfresco restaurant where an old lady taps me on the shoulder, then points upwards while asking me if I am interested in looking at hand-made lace and mantillas. The workroom upstairs is full of small, elderly Spanish ladies dressed in black from head to toe, all working on highly intricate embroidery. Pedro buys me a wonderful black hand-embroidered silk wrap and a lace mantilla, both of which are absolute bargains considering all the beautiful work which has gone into making them. These past few days we've spent together have been perfect. It's how I dreamed our life together would be.

267

The following day is even better. We play Jai Alai. I absolutely love it! It's a bit like squash except there are only three walls at the front, back and left-hand side. On the right-hand side, you just have to keep the ball inside of the line. Jai Alai is more a matter of brute force than touch. The *cancha* is as long as a tennis court and you have to hit the ball on the far wall without letting it bounce. The two big Basques that we play doubles against are surprised that I can manage it so easily. Little did these boys know that I'd had a substantial amount of practice hitting tennis balls long distances with notes in them from the Narrabeen high girls over to their boyfriends at the twin school during the lunch hour.

Jai Alai, which was invented by the Basques, means "merry festival" in their language, but our game is anything but light-hearted. It is hard, fast and furious—and our opponents take it very seriously. It is obvious they would not care to lose to a woman. As it turns out, Pedro is a much better Jai Alai player than he is at tennis so we manage to tie the match. The two Basque boys decide not to play a decider.

Pedro and I have been to watch a professional Jai Alai game in the centre of Madrid which is played with a *cesta-punta* strapped to the players' arms and very fast, small hard balls which speed through the air at around 200 ks per hour. Funnily enough bookmakers took bets by tossing up tennis balls with splits in them in which the punters placed their bets. I had to laugh. For our game of Jai Alai though, we play with tennis racquets and balls, which is a lot easier than playing with the traditional equipment.

The Wilson Cup
Memorial Drive Park
ADELAIDE

The Wilson Cup is an important under 19 girls interstate team competition held once a year, before the Australian Open. I am the number one player for NSW and am playing in both the singles and the doubles. I find it harrowing having to play the top girls in each state twice a day in singles, then back up for the doubles. By the third day I am completely stressed out. I have the runs. There's nothing left in my stomach. Only butterflies. Mary Horton, our team captain is calling me to go on. It's the first time she's in charge. She wants to win really badly. But I can't take any more pressure. I put enough on myself. She's knocking on the loo door and telling me that I must come out now or we'll be forfeited. I've no alternative.

Chapter 58

ME PARECE QUE ESTOY EN ESTADO

I haven't had my periods since the middle of August, and it is nearly the end of September, which is more than six weeks. I also feel crook every morning. Nor do I feel better later in the day or at night when I cook dinner, especially if it is anything greasy. The only thing I feel like eating is yoghurt. When I tell Pedro, although he doesn't appear to be as excited as I am, he says he'll ask around about doctors at the Chamartin Tennis Club. He is recommended to Dr Maranon, an obstetrician, and makes an appointment.

"From all accounts, senora, it looks like you are pregnant," Dr Maranon tells me, "but I will confirm it in a couple of days when I get the tests back."

Doctors' procedures are never pleasant. They also always run late. So here I am stuck in the waiting room, getting more anxious by the minute. The copies of *Hola* I find on the glass table in front of me hardly distract as they are so old that half the people in them are probably dead by now. When I finally do get in to see the doctor, I am so nervous I have to bite my bottom lip hard, so I don't burst into tears. The doctor tells me to take off all my clothes and put on a thin cotton gown, which opens down the back. I tremble as I get up onto the examination table and place my feet into the stirrups on either side. Pedro certainly doesn't help. When the doctor draws the curtains closed, I hear him stomp out of the doctor's office, slamming the door behind him.

What follows I do not want to even think about. How is the baby ever going to come out of such a small space, when it hurts like hell with just a couple of fingers in a plastic glove? What a nightmare! I have to grab the examination table because my knees buckle when I get off it. I don't know why I was so keen to have a baby. My hormones have overridden every other thought in my mind and feeling in my body. I certainly hadn't contemplated this particular aspect of having a baby. The doctor asks me a few more questions and then tells me that I must only think beautiful thoughts, because whatever I think will transfer to the baby and will affect its wellbeing.

Doctor Maranon then goes on to recommend having a glass of red wine with each meal to keep up my red corpuscles. Does he mean breakfast too, I wonder, but don't dare ask! This is certainly a bit different from the advice in a newspaper article which Mum sent me recently headed "Nine Months of Anxiety" which gave dire warnings to pregnant women about drinking any alcohol whatsoever. Dr Maranon then pats me on the shoulder and gives me some information about a course I can do about having a baby, which is run by a Russian company.

"This course covers the Pavlov method, otherwise known as psychoprophylaxis, which is a very effective technique developed in the Soviet Union to prepare women for childbirth without anaesthetic, by psychological training, physical conditioning and breathing exercises," he adds.

This will hopefully be some kind of help, because I really don't have a clue what to expect. Nobody I can think of has had a baby or if they have, I haven't really paid any attention.

Outside the surgery I find Pedro smoking one of his dreadful smelly cigars and striding up and down. Smoke appears to be coming out of his head as well as his mouth. He is furious.

"Bloody pervert," he says. "That's the last time you are going to see that mongrel doctor."

I gather that the preceding examination is normal practice but can't see any point in telling Pedro at this particular point in time, when he is in such an irrational mood. I am a little surprised to say the least. I can't believe he would think that he has anything to worry about with Doctor Maranon who definitely is no oil painting. In fact, he is a very typical-looking, middle-aged Spanish bloke, short, portly and swarthy and at least 50. I am also absolutely positive that in his occupation he has seen so many vaginas that he would be sick to death of the sight of them.

Dr Maranon rings a few days later. "Senora Rivera de Flores? Good news! You are definitely pregnant."

Immediately I panic. Is it such good news? There is no way out now. But I can't wait to let Mum and Dad know. When I ring to tell them the news they are very excited. It will be their first grandchild. They tell me that they are going to come over to Spain for the birth. I am so excited about finally being pregnant that I go out and buy a whole wardrobe of maternity dresses.

My only dilemma now is how to broach Pedro about his table manners during Mum and Dad's visit. They are always so particular about this kind of thing. I don't know what their reaction is going be to dunking bread in the sauce to mop it up, scooping peas instead of squashing them on the back of the fork, not to mention leaving the knife and fork on the plate in such a haphazard manner that they look like they had just fallen there from the sky when he has finished eating.

It's an emergency

A siren is blaring and an ambulance is blocking the entrance to the Strathfield Lawn Tennis Club when I arrive to play my match in the Metropolitan Grasscourt Championships. Two men are pushing a stretcher followed by Dr Bartlett and my brother. "Dad had a stroke on match point," John gasps. "I was playing against Dr Bartlett's son, John. Lucky that Dad was sitting right next to John's father. He treated him straight away." The ambulance is taking Dad to hospital. But we all end up back at home. Even though he's nearly at death's door, Dad refuses to go to hospital.

Chapter 59

LAS TETILLAS, EL BATIDO DE FRESAS Y UNA TARTA DE MANZANA

I am beside myself with worry. I have examined my nipples carefully to see if there are holes in them and can't see any even after a closer inspection in the mirror. None! How on earth is the milk going to come out? I hope they are not going to have to put holes in them because they are so sore already that I couldn't bear the thought of needles going into them. I try to think about Snow Boots our cat and wonder whether Mum had undertaken any kind of procedure with her. But maybe cats are different.

The only thing I can do is to ask my friend Joyce what happens. She's had three babies and is bound to know. When I finally summon up the courage, Joyce falls back on the sofa and bursts into fits of laughter. In fact, she seems unable to stop.

"My jaws are aching so much I can't stand it," she squeezes out.

I don't find it funny at all. In fact, I have to work very hard to hold back my tears.

"That's the funniest thing I have ever heard," she gasps.

I can't hold out any longer. The tears spill out and roll down my cheeks. Joyce puts her arm around me.

"The milk just comes out," she ends up saying. "No need for holes. When you are ready to feed the baby, there won't be a problem, I promise."

"Please don't tell anyone about this, Joyce," I plead. I am really embarrassed.

Strawberry milkshake, strawberry milkshake, strawberry milkshake! Strawberry milkshake is all I can think about. I have an unbelievably strong craving for strawberry milkshakes and it has been going on all week. I don't even like strawberry milkshakes normally. In fact, I have never been that keen on milk in general. Having lived near a dairy as a small child I consumed so much milk, not to mention those milk puddings every night, that I'd gotten well and truly sick of it. Then there was the milk we were forced to drink each morning at school after it had been sitting out in the hot sun for hours and had gone sour.

I decide it must be one of those food cravings women get when they're pregnant that I've read about in the *Women's Own* magazine. Yesterday I nearly died of frustration because they ran out of strawberry flavouring at the coffee shop down the road. But they've promised faithfully they'll have some more today. I am busting my boiler this morning because the shop doesn't open for another hour. But there is nothing else to do but wait it out.

A few days later, all I can think about is apple pie, apple pie, apple pie. And I don't mean the apple pies at boarding school which had pieces of core left in that we all swore blind were the cook's fingernails. Nor the ones that Mum used to make with crumble on top, although they were delicious. The ones I am thinking about I am fervently gazing at in the *reposteria* window just down the road from our apartment. They have finely sliced apples encrusted with caramelised sugar on top and confectioner's custard cream underneath. I've tried to restrain myself. I am sure they are not the best thing to eat during pregnancy and will no doubt result in my poor child having the most terrible sweet tooth. But I can't resist any longer. In no time at all, I am coming out of the shop, pie in hand, my mouth watering in anticipation, a smile on my face.

Back in our apartment, I polish off the whole pie in one sitting. Afterwards I feel sick, very sick!

I'm learning to meditate

I try not to giggle but it's hard. The sight of Dad walking up Myrtle Street, Crows Nest, in his safari suit, with a large white handkerchief, a piece of fruit and a flower at the ready for his induction ceremony is almost too much to bear. Dad has always been interested in alternative ideas and therapies particularly when they offer health benefits and especially if they promise to lower his blood pressure. Mum won't have a bar of any of these ideas and refuses to go with him. That's why I am here. We've already attended lectures on Transcendental Meditation by the Maharishi Mahesh Yogi. Today we receive our mantras.

When I come out I'm busting to know if Dad's word is the same as mine, but I don't say anything. We have been told to keep them a secret. I want mine to work. I button my lips.

Chapter 60

UNA VISITA

I am beside myself with excitement because my brother, John, is coming to visit. As Harry Hopman no longer accompanies the Australian men's team, John has been travelling with his doubles partner, Phil Dent. He has been playing in an indoor tournament at the Royal Lawn Tennis Club in Stockholm and has a week off before he goes to play in the Grand Prix Super Series tournament in Johannesburg. I haven't seen him in ages and am looking forward to hearing how he is getting on with his tennis career. I can also hardly wait to catch up on all the news and gossip from back home. Not that it will be easy. Men are never forthcoming with what most women consider to be of the utmost importance. I know I will have to pry it out of him. I am also looking forward to speaking English. Once again I feel like a fat lady on a diet deprived of her favourite chocolate cake. When I am out with Pedro and his friends and they talk in Spanish, by the end of the day, my head feels like it is going to burst! In desperation I've been attending a Bible studies group with the Episcopalians during the week, just to be with people who speak English, as well as going to church on Sunday at the Eurobuilding. But in the end, I decide that the Bible group is perhaps carrying things a bit too far—especially as I'm not even religious.

John will be surprised when he sees me, as I am now visibly pregnant and have a noticeable bump. I can also feel the baby kicking around inside me. I am finding it really hard being so far away from family and friends now I am pregnant. I have no idea what is going on or about to happen next and I'm too embarrassed to ask Joyce anything else after my last effort.

The day after his arrival, Pedro, John and I drive to Segovia. We have the most gorgeous and hilarious time. Segovia, with its twisting cobbled alleyways, lovely old Romanesque churches, ancient buildings and famous aqueduct, is one of my favourite cities. Whenever I am there, I can just imagine Queen Isabella and Columbus on one of the *palacio* balconies, discussing the finances he will need to discover America.

We eat lunch at the Meson de Candido, my favourite restaurant in Segovia, which has been run by the same family since 1786. John gets stuck right into the food. I can't believe how much he manages to eat, especially as he has the white bean soup, a hearty meal in itself, as an entrée. We all have the house specialty for mains, *cochinillo* (baby suckling pig), which is so deliciously tender that it can be cut with a china plate. I really do love the sensation when I get a piece of meat in my mouth. It melts in the most satisfying way before sliding silkily down my throat. It is certainly nothing like the crumbed pork cutlets that Mum used to serve up every now and again "for a change". They always needed a very good chew.

On the way back to Madrid, we stop at another of my favourite places, La Granja de San Ildefonso, which was purchased by King Phillip V from the monks in 1719 after his nearby summer palace at Valsain burned to a shell. It is only about eleven kilometers from Segovia, a truly magical place, its beautiful palace surrounded by gardens and fountains, with the snow-capped Sierra de Guadarrama mountains in the background. We stroll around the gardens, which were built for King Felipe V, who was so envious of his grandfather King Louis XIV's Garden at Versailles that he spent twenty years trying to replicate them. Then we go on a guided tour of the inside of the palace.

There are seven of us in the group, including a very serious-faced guide, who is dressed in period costume. Replete with a pleated collar, he looks like he's stepped right off the pages of a history book. As we head off on the tour, it starts to get really funny, for me anyway! As we enter the first of the dazzling, high-ceilinged rooms containing the most beautiful XVII century tapestries, someone in our group lets off such a ripsnorter of a "silent deadly bomber", that it permeates the whole air space, hardly leaving a speck of breathable air. I can't help myself. I scurry to the far corner of the room where I discover that there is nothing worse than being pregnant, and as full as a goog with food, while trying to stifle a fit of giggles.

My stomach aches but when I look around at the guide, he doesn't even move a muscle. His face is like it is set in cement. I can't believe that he doesn't smell anything because it is an absolute knockout! Then I casually glance at the rest of the group. These guys are all candidates for an Academy Award unless their sinuses are stuffed up. Not one of them shows the least sign of being the bombardier, or even for that matter, smelling anything malodorous, which makes it even worse for me. I honestly feel like I am going to burst at the seams. As we move from room to room, the perpetrator does encore after encore, and still there is absolutely no reaction from either the guide or the men in the group. I glance questioningly at John and Pedro but get no response. By the third room, I just can't take any more, and am forced to hightail it out to the garden, where I break into an uncontrollable fit of giggles. I just laugh and laugh and laugh until my jaws ache and my sides feel like they are going to split.

On the way back to Madrid in the car, when I question Pedro and John, they both emphatically deny that it was them.

"But you must have smelled something. It was bloody foul," I insist.

Jeez, not a bloody word! To be fair I don't think Pedro quite understands the finer points of what I am talking about. I don't know how to say fart in Spanish. I just have to make do with the actions and sound effects, which set me off laughing uncontrollably again. And as for John, our family has always been one of deniers, always blaming poor Jazz, the dog, even after he'd been dead a considerable number of years.

Up, up and away

*Any minute I think I am going to wake up and find myself back in my bed at home. Instead, I am stretched across three seats on a plane headed for Singapore. There are only nine passengers. I am travelling with John Bartlett. Dad found out that he was going to play in the tournament in Monte Carlo as well, and arranged with Dr Bartlett, John's father, for us to travel together. John Bartlett comes from Wollongong and has led an even more sheltered life than me. I don't think I have **ever** seen him without at least one—and usually both—of his parents in tow.*

Chapter 61

NO ME GUSTA NADA LOS JUEGOS

Before he leaves, John gives Pedro and me a Scrabble set as a wedding present. It is certainly much better than the one we played with as children. It comes in a very elegant case with fine wooden pieces for the letters. Nor is the board made from thick cardboard—the border of the playing area is in rosewood.

I don't like board games. I find them tedious and still vividly remember all the arguments we had as children over games of Snakes and Ladders and Monopoly. However, Pedro is very keen to play. He thinks it will help improve his English. So we start our first game. It takes forever, because Pedro insists on playing in English, and practically goes through the entire dictionary before putting down a word. Consequently, we don't get anywhere near finishing the game and have to leave the board set up down one end of the dining table.

Four days later, the game is still going on. I knew I didn't like board games. At the best of times they are too slow and test my patience to the absolute limit. But this particular game is death defyingly slow. Pedro is moving even more slowly than usual tonight because it looks like I am going to win fairly soon. But just as I am about to place my winning word down, he grabs the whole board and tips it up!

I can really feel the baby moving around a lot, especially when I play tennis. It is like there are two of us when I run, one of me goes one way and the other stays put, despite the maternity corset that Doctor Maranon recommended I wear. I am beginning to think I won't be able to play too much longer. But Pedro has decided he wants to play tennis with me and there's no getting out of it. I can see from the look in his eyes that he thinks this is going to be his big moment. That at last he will be able to beat me. I know he's been down at the club having lessons with the pro all week.

Poor Pedro. He just doesn't get it. I've played tennis since I was seven. It is like breathing to me. And unfortunately for him, it is just not in my nature to let anyone win a game, unless they do so by their own merit. When he comes out of the change room dressed for the event in shiny white, I do feel a bit sorry for him—almost. The word has spread around the club and a crowd has gathered around the court, whispering and tittering behind their palms.

Pedro has obviously been working on some tactics with the pro. At every opportunity he attempts to drop the ball short over the net thinking that in my current condition, I won't be able to get it. He doesn't have a show even if I do turn out to be a bit slower than usual, as he unfortunately doesn't have the necessary touch. He also telegraphs what he is going to do. I easily get to the short balls and bang them away for winners. At 4–0, he is practically frothing at the mouth. At 5–0 the crowd starts to move away, a wise decision. At 6–0, 5–0 Pedro decides he doesn't want to play anymore and stomps off the court.

Fortunately, I've driven over in my own car. I don't think I would be good for a lift back home. I linger at the club in the hope that he'll cool down.

But as soon as I come in the front door I can smell more trouble. Pedro, I can see, has been busy doing something in the bedroom. We'd been unable to find a double bed big enough for the two of us, as we were both so much taller than most Spanish couples, so Pedro bought two single ones and sewed the mattresses together. Now he has the scissors out and is snipping the stitches. When he finishes, he pulls the two divans apart. I wonder what I've done this time. I guess I will find out soon. I put the kettle on, take a deep breath and wait.

A few moments later, Pedro comes into the kitchen waving a newspaper in front of my nose. When he finally stops, I can see there is a picture of me in it, taken on the day I'd gone to watch the tennis tournament at the Puerta de Hierro. The caption underneath reads "SUSANA ALEXANDER-RIVERA DE FLORES—TENIS STAR AUSTRALIAN ESTA JUGANDO UN NUEVO JUEGO" (Australian Tennis Star is playing a new game). The article goes on to say how I'd recently married Pedro and am expecting our first child.

"I do not want my wife's picture in the paper," Pedro roars, waving it in my face once again.

I can't quite understand where he is coming from. I'd have thought he would be proud of me. They certainly have some very peculiar ways here in Spain. But what can I do?

Singapore

When I step out of the airport I am instantly bathed in sweat. JB decides not to come with me. He is worried about missing the plane for Nice. But I might never come this way again. I hire a taxi and get him to drive me around town. There are more bicycles than cars. Trishaws are the main mode of transport used to ferry people. Rubbish-filled water is gushing down each side of the streets, which are lined with rickety market stalls and eateries, dilapidated timber houses, exotic Asian temples interspersed with lush tropical gardens. A monkey leaps across parked-car roofs then eats a banana in the gutter.

*So **very** different to Sydney.*

Everyone is Asian except me.

Chapter 62

NO PUEDO MAS - ME VOY

Morning sickness hasn't stopped at the end of the first three months like it was supposed to. Nor has it confined itself to the mornings. I feel sick all day. Some days I really wonder what I have gotten myself into. Have I made a dreadful mistake? I decide that I'm definitely not one of those women who bloom when they are pregnant. I'm really not enjoying the experience at all and in fact feel quite cross most of the time.

Pedro doesn't help. My pregnancy has obviously pushed his emotional buttons. With all his temperamental explosions and eruptions, he leaves Mount Etna for dead. I am now onto my fourth obstetrician, Dr Rohrbach, because Pedro became upset with the other three as soon as they made me take my clothes off. I refuse to let him come to this last appointment and just as well, because Dr Rohrbach is extremely charming as well as being drop dead gorgeous. He is pleased with my progress but a bit surprised that I'm not putting on any weight and in fact have steadily been losing it. I am not surprised in the least. After all the over-eating that went on during our honeymoon, I am sure that there is just some kind of redistribution taking place.

Things are going downhill on the home front. When I get home Pedro is not happy at all. And neither am I. I am at the end of my tether. He is so unbearably obnoxious yet again that I decide I can't take it anymore. I pack all my things into my two battered old suitcases for the fourteenth time. But this time I am deadly serious. I take everything downstairs and put it into the car ready to go. I've come to the conclusion that Pedro is impossible to live with. He has once again boiled over about absolutely nothing at all— this time about a small amount of dust he detected on the bookcase, when he'd told me previously that doing the housework wasn't my job anyway. It didn't matter, once again he starts ranting, raving, flinging his arms about and stamping his feet.

Then he goes into the bathroom, slams the door and stays there for a good hour. When he comes out, looking immaculately groomed as usual, his lips are pursed tight. How long will the "no talkies' last this time, I wonder. His record so far has been three weeks! Thank goodness we don't have any neighbours. Whatever would they make of it! Would he give them a dispensation and talk to them in the hallway, or would they also be included in the silent treatment? I've tried every conceivable tactic to counteract his behaviour. I've ignored him, yelled back at him and sweet-talked him—without success.

Now I've finally had enough. Pedro realises that perhaps he's gone one step too far and that this time I mean it. He follows me down to the garage and watches as I put the last of my things in the boot, get into the front seat and put the key in the ignition. I can see that he is almost in tears. It is as though he's metamorphosed into a different person. He starts to talk to me in a very charming, romantic and passionate voice wooing, flattering and enticing me back into his loving arms, which he is holding out in front of him while telling me that he can't live without me. What can I do? My passport is in his safe, I have just over 500 pesetas in my pocket, and I am five and half months pregnant. I can see myself getting halfway across France and running out of money and petrol. I would certainly hate to have to rely on my schoolgirl French to extricate myself from that kind of predicament. It would be way too big a stretch.

Pedro carries all my things back upstairs.

I am at a loss as to what to do. Mum and Dad are no doubt, at this very moment, on their way to Canada for my brother John's wedding and after that are due to fly to Spain. I've no way of contacting them. Not that they could do anything mid-air.

I'm in France. Oooh la la! What a gas!

*When I step out into the Nice airport lounge, things don't look **too** different. It's only when I see people close up that they don't look the same. Nor do they speak the same. In my best schoolgirl French, I ask, "Ou est le train pour Monte Carlo?, while fervently praying that the answer is not going to be too long or complicated. Fortunately, it is only "la bas" and the little French bloke I ask points at the same time. Somehow we manage to buy our tickets and get on the right train. I spend the entire journey with my nose pressed up against the carriage window. I want to imprint every frame in my memory.*

Chapter 63

UNA VERDADERA SORPRESA

I feel like I've been run over by a Mack truck. My whole body hurts and I notice that there are two wet patches on my nightie at boob level. When I look around, it is like I am back in the dormitory at boarding school, except that everyone is a lot older. Then it all floods back.

It is as though it is a dream, or rather a nightmare! It begins as most Sundays do. I have gone to the Episcopalian church service at the Hotel Eurobuilding, but halfway through the service when I stand up to sing, I feel water trickling down my leg. My face burns with embarrassment, as I race down the aisle and out the door. Everyone turns to look at me. I can't believe it! I've wet myself. How embarrassing is that! I hope desperately that this isn't going to happen all the time during the last three months of my pregnancy.

When I get home and tell Pedro what has happened he thinks I should ring the doctor. But I can't see any point, because I am only just over six months pregnant. It is way too early for anything to happen yet. So we sit down to lunch, and although it is my favourite, *pescado con ajillo*, I don't really feel hungry and hardly manage to eat a thing. After lunch, Pedro insists on a roll in the hay. If the truth be told, sex is the last thing on my mind. I am not one of those women I've read about in the *Women's Own*, who can't get enough sex when they're pregnant. My sex drive has all but disappeared! And anyway, how could anyone feel sexy with boobs that feel like boils when they are touched, skin that continually breaks out, and hair that is lank and greasy and impossible to manage? Not to mention a swollen stomach!

Pedro certainly isn't worried about not climaxing now, and it is rather a vigorous affair. Straight afterwards, I have to race to the toilet, and when I look in the bowl I notice my urine is tinged with red. When I tell Pedro, this time he insists on ringing the doctor, who says it sounds like my waters must have broken, and directs us to come straight to the hospital. I don't know anything about *waters* because I've only been to two prenatal classes and we haven't gotten up to that part so far. In the first week's session, we watched short films of Russian women having babies utilising the Pavlov method. Halfway through, Pedro felt sick and had to leave. To tell the truth, I felt a bit sick myself. It certainly wasn't a pleasant sight watching birth after birth, particularly as the sight of blood always makes me feel queasy, but I don't have any choice. I am stuck with it. The next week during the second session, our giggly group of expectant mums took it in turns to bathe large, plastic dolls.

We drive across town to the Anglo-American hospital. After an examination by the doctor on duty, I am told that I am in the last stage of labour.

"That can't be right!" I tell him. "What about all those agonising labour pains I'm supposed to have?"

Why only the other day, when I ran into Senora Gonzales from down the street, she'd given me a ball to ball description of the hour after hour of agony she experienced with the birth of each of her six children. What I found hard to understand is why the hell she kept backing up for more.

"This is definitely the case, senora," the doctor insists and instructs the nurse to wheel me into the delivery room.

At this stage, I have a major panic attack. I have absolutely no idea what is going to happen next, nor what I have to do, so I send Pedro back home for the course notes.

"*Y date bloody prisa*," (Step on it) I yell at his back as he disappears around the corner.

No sooner does he leave, than they wheel me down the corridor and into the delivery room. It isn't a good scene. Before I know it, my feet are in those dreaded stirrups once again. I am certainly glad I can't see myself, because although I am scared witless, I am cringing with embarrassment. There is a team of at least six people down the wrong end of me, examining the situation while they wait for my obstetrician to arrive. However, things start to move ahead quickly so the doctor in charge tells me that they will have to make do without him, and although I still don't feel any of those dreadful labour pains at all, it is certainly a very tight squeeze when the baby starts to come out.

After the most excruciating ten minutes I've experienced in my whole life, which feels like going to the toilet after not having been for at least six months and six stitches, my baby is born. I can't believe it! Pedro is certainly going to get a surprise when he gets back with my notes. It is then that the debonair Dr Rohrbach puts in an appearance, apologising profusely for his late arrival, telling me he has just got off the plane after attending a medical conference in Switzerland. But even in my current state of disarray, I find his tale a bit far-fetched. From his tanned face, peeling nose and the happy smile on his face he looks more like he's been cavorting on the ski slopes rather than cloistered inside a conference facility.

"The good news," he tells me proudly, "is that I've brought you back a three-month supply of the birth control pill, which is not available here in Spain."

I smile weakly, but to tell the truth, sex is certainly the last thing on my mind after this little stoush.

I am only able to look at my new baby for a moment before the nurse whips him away.

"He's so tiny—just under three pounds," she tells me on the run-through.

In the brief squiz I manage to grab as he is rushed out the door and down the hallway, he looks like one of those skinned rabbits I'd seen hanging up in the kitchen at the restaurant in El Pardo. His skin is translucent, he is bald and very much smaller than the big Spanish babies I'd seen earlier in the day, who are born with wads of thick black curly hair, and if they are girls, their ears are pierced. I don't even get to touch him, let alone make sure he has all his fingers and toes. But at least he is a boy, which is a major relief. The doctor tells me that he is going to be placed in a humidicrib because he is so small and his lungs are under developed and that he will probably have to stay there for at least a month, that is, if he lives.

When Pedro returns, his mind goes into such a complete whirl when he is told that the baby has already been born, that I decide to seize the moment to persuade him to call him Alexander Jon instead of one of the long Spanish names he has in mind.

Everything has just happened too quickly. I'm in total shock. I feel unprepared emotionally and psychologically. The wondrous feelings of newly acquired motherhood and instant maternal love for my tiny baby, which Mum has told me about, have simply not happened.

Well not at this stage, anyway.

I'm in Monte Carlo!

Monte Carlo Country Club overlooks the Mediterranean Sea and is gorgeous! It's my first tournament in Europe but I almost don't get to play. Another, not-so-gracious Australian woman tennis player tells the tournament organisers that I'm not good enough even though I only just lost to her at the Manly Seaside in a three-set match. I have to put up a fight. Fortunately, I've brought letters of recommendation from Dunlop.

I'm staying in a pensione just up the street from the club. My room with its high ceilings, dark rose-coloured carpet and large old-fashioned furniture is quite the loveliest room I've ever stayed in. Every morning the smell of fresh bread wafts into my room from the wonderful market right underneath my window. I love French food. Even the vegetables taste good. As for the sauces, they are to die for.

I only just lose in the open to an Italian girl who lobs and drop shots every ball alternatively, which on these slow en-tout-cas courts is a nightmare! I win the Junior girls final against Judy Salome 6–4, 6–3. It attracts a large crowd. And not just for the tennis. We are both young and gorgeous.

297

Chapter 64

AHORA SOY UNA MADRE

The next morning, the nurse comes in with a strange-looking contraption "for expressing milk," she explains. She says that breast milk will really help Alex's immune system. It is as awful and as painful a procedure as I imagine. My breasts are so sore, the last thing I feel like doing, is pumping at them. I also feel very undignified, like one of those cows I'd seen going around on the Rotalactor when I'd been on an excursion in primary school. I have to stop myself from going "moo".

I'm not allowed to touch Alex in case of germs and can only peer at him through the glass window. Quite frankly, I can't see why I have more germs than the nurses. One thing I do notice is that Alex has blue eyes. The matron tells me that they'll stay that way. When I point this out to Pedro, he immediately jumps to the conclusion that I really must have had an affair with that blue-eyed French physio back in Fuengirola, and this is the result. I only manage to calm him down when I remind him that my father has blue eyes, as does his brother Luiz, *and* Ramona, his mother.

It's funny! I don't feel like a mother at all. Maybe it is because it has all been so sudden and I haven't been able to hold or touch Alex. The whole situation feels unreal. Or perhaps I was in the loo when God handed out the motherly, nurturing personality traits. Or possibly I take after Grandma Alexander and "lack maternal feelings". I wonder if that kind of thing is hereditary. Mum certainly doesn't lack maternal feelings. She's dotty about babies. She always wanting to nurse and goo-goo ga-ga at all babies on sight and starts knitting tiny garments as soon as she finds out anyone she knows is pregnant. Dad also adores babies. He can never resist picking them up. In the end Mum had to dress him in safari suits for work because the dry-cleaning bill was getting too expensive from babies puking down the front of his dress suits, shirts and silk ties.

The day I come out of hospital is a huge relief. I can't stand hospitals, particularly the smell, which in my opinion is even worse than doctors' surgeries. One more day in there and I would have been in search of some razor blades. Although I am sad to leave little Alex behind still in the humidicrib, I know he is in good hands, much better than in my inexperienced ones.

When I get home our apartment looks like a bomb has hit it. Alvaro, Pedro's ancient cousin from Bonar, who smokes like a chimney, has been staying with him. There are overflowing ashtrays on every available surface. There is also a box full of empty wine bottles near the door. As cousin Alvaro also likes to have garlic soup for breakfast, the whole apartment reeks of garlic and sweat. Alvaro obviously isn't one to worry too much about having regular showers or use deodorant. I can see that the two of them have been having a jolly old time while I've been slugging it out at the hospital.

I find it hard to believe that they have been living in such a mess, when Pedro is normally so fastidious. I wonder where Jomey is. She's most probably gone on strike.

The first few weeks pass by in a haze of expressing milk twice a day and rushing it over to the hospital. Fortunately, Alex is steadily putting on weight. Pedro is in a total dither and not much help at all. Thank goodness he decided to ship Goz back to the country with cousin Alvaro. Although I will miss him I don't think I could handle any additional strain. Mum and Dad are arriving very soon and just as well — I am nearly at my wits' end. I desperately need help, advice and support.

I send Pedro to meet them. They don't dare ask whether our baby is a boy or a girl, because they'd already heard from John how desperate Pedro is to have a boy. It is as if his whole manhood depends on it and in the Spanish culture that is fairly close to the truth. Instead, ever tactful, they ask what we've decided to call the baby. Confusion ensues because there is no X in Spanish, so Pedro's Alex, sounds like Alice. I have a little giggle to myself when I imagine the scenario. They somehow manage to get the confusion straightened out in the end and are very relieved, as I am. that the baby is a boy.

Pedro drops Mum and Dad off at the short-term rental we've managed to find for them in one of the buildings in Calle Doctor Fleming for the three months that they'll be here. I can hardly wait to catch up with the latest—in particular I'm dying to hear about John's wedding in Toronto. After their sojourn in Madrid, Mum and Dad are going to England to watch him play at Wimbledon.

A month has passed, Alex now weighs five pounds and I'm informed that I can take him home from the hospital. When I pick him up the following morning, the doctor gives me a very strict warning about how fragile he is. I am only too aware of how Alex feels, he isn't the only one. I feel fragile too!

"He's still not breathing very well," the doctor tells me.

His dire warning succeeds in turning me into a very cautious driver and an hysterical mother. Every night, I am awake practically the whole night, wetting my finger and putting it in front of Alex's nose, to check whether he is still breathing.

Thank goodness Mum comes around to help when I get home that first day. I am very much in need of her support while I have my first go at bottle-feeding Alex. Alex is on a formula called Nectomil, which is made from goat's milk and honey, because it turns out that he is allergic to cows' milk. I have to intersperse it with breast-milk feeds. The doctor has recommended that I continue expressing milk as long as I can. It is a case of the blind leading the blind because Mum had breastfed all three of us for six months plus and has about as much experience with bottles and formulas as I do. Nectomil, unlike my breast milk, is so thick we can't get it to go through the teat properly. It is so frustrating! First the hole in the teat is too small and nothing will come out. Then when we make it bigger, it spurts out all over the place. Meantime, Alex is starving and yelling his lungs out, which certainly doesn't help matters. Panic ensues!

I burst into tears, and Mum is pretty close to crying too, but stoic that she is, manages to keep a lid on it. We make several trips back and forth to the *farmacia* for more teats. That first day seems endless! Alex is still so small he is on one-and-a-half-hourly feeds. No sooner do I feed him, get his wind up, change his nappy and sterilise the bottle than we have to start over. There is hardly a moment's rest. Eventually to our great relief, we succeed, but both of us are totally worn out with the effort and desperate for a cup of tea. Thank God Mum is here as I definitely wouldn't be able to cope by myself.

Mum and I finally manage to sit down for that cup of tea. We've just finished giving Alex a bath in the kitchen sink, with Mum holding him while I soap him up then tip cups of water over him. He is certainly a lot smaller than those plastic dolls I practised on at the course. The tea poured, Mum is now wiggling in her seat and appears to be extremely uncomfortable about something.

"There's certainly more to having children than a quick root in a drunken stupor," she says with a laugh. Mum is always ready with one of her country expressions for any occasion. She then starts telling me how sorry she is that she's never managed to get around to explaining to me about the "birds and the bees". "But I guess you know it all now?" she adds, looking decidedly relieved.

Mum has never been much good discussing anything about sex. I remember only too well how embarrassed she was when I got my periods.

Although Alex is progressing well on the formula, Mum and Dad are both very keen for me to breastfeed. I'm not quite so keen on the idea myself, although it would make night feeds a lot easier, I suppose. So while Mum, Alex and I are in the bedroom, Dad proceeds to issue us with instructions from the kitchen. Alex shows no interest whatsoever in my proffered nipple, and starts yelling. As usual, he is starving and is not used to any delays. Then Dad comes up with the brilliant idea of putting honey on my nipples in order to entice him. Alex is too used to getting his feed easily, so after he licks all the honey off and makes a couple of slurps without much of a result, he loses interest. We both end up in a sticky mess. I decide to stick with expressing the milk and giving it to him from the bottle. I'm glad! I know Mum got great joy and satisfaction from breastfeeding, but to be honest I don't like the feel of it at all. It's obviously not everyone's cup of tea.

My maternal feelings still haven't surfaced and I'm finding it hard to believe that Alex is really mine. I also feel like death warmed up as I didn't sleep a wink last night between the feeds, and worrying that Alex will stop breathing. Now Pedro has decided to relegate us to the lounge room sofa. He complains that he can't get any sleep because Alex is screaming every night, starting in the late afternoon until one or two in the morning. The only way to placate him is to play classical music very loudly which, when combined with the screams, sounds like some mad Italian opera. Pedro isn't the only one who isn't getting any sleep.

I feel frantic, frustrated, worried, exhausted, confused, guilty and totally inadequate. At last we manage to get an appointment with a pediatrician. It turns out that Alex has colic, which is why he screams after all his feeds.

Le Country Club - Aix en Provence.

I'm invited to play in Aix-en-Provence. The invitation is a ripper—impossible to resist—it includes my transport to Aix, my accommodation and food. It also means I can delay my arrival in England where I've heard that it is still very cold and wet at this time of the year.

My room in the elegant old hotel is absolutely gorgeous! It's the bridal suite. The bath, which is on top of a platform, is big enough for four people and has gold taps and fittings. The country club where the tournament is being held is luxurious and the food is to die for.

After I eat dinner at La Rotunde I walk along Le Cours Mirabeau. I hear "Sitting on the Dock of the Bay", one of my favourite songs coming out of a nightclub called "La Boite Rose". I end up dancing the night away with my new best friends, Claude and Jean Paul, who are studying here in Aix.

Chapter 65

Vuelvo a jugar al tenis

Alex is just over six weeks old and is sleeping through the night now that we've remedied his colic. I am keen to get back to tennis. I am due to play in the Madrid Championships in a couple of weeks so I need to get a bit of practice in. I also have really missed getting a good sweat up over the last few months, so I've arranged to have my first hit at the Club de Campo with Estela Benavides.

I feel exhausted just getting there. I am still expressing milk, which really takes a lot out of me even though I'm eating like a horse. And with all the paraphernalia I have to organise and cart with me whenever I go anywhere with Alex, it feels like I've played a hard three-set match before I even hit the first ball.

No sooner do I place Alex in his carry cot at the side of the court than he starts screaming blue murder. Having only just fed, burped him *and* changed his nappy, I can't imagine what on earth could be wrong. Estela is a bit annoyed at the delay. She hasn't had any children yet and doesn't understand about babies at all. However, she has just married and as she's a Catholic, no doubt it won't be too long before the patter of little feet will be heard in their household as there is no birth control available in Spain. I haven't as yet started taking the pills that Dr Rohrbach managed to sneak in for me from Switzerland, because I've been stalling any renewal of marital relations with Pedro. A roll in the hay is the last thing on my mind at the moment. I definitely don't want to fall pregnant again straight away, especially with our relationship in such a state of disarray.

The tournament, which is held at the Club de Campo, is grinding. My energy is still very much depleted, as I'm still expressing milk. I only just manage to beat Monica Alvarez Mon, one of my students, in the final in a torrid three-set match. Later, when I am playing a mixed doubles match with Alfonso, the coach from the Puerta de Hierro tennis club, Pedro arrives. I can see that I have done something wrong because Pedro is striding up and down at the side of the court, puffing one cigar after the other. When I get off the court he goes absolutely berserk because I have played doubles with another man—even though Alfonso is old, married and has four teenage children. He huffs back into his car, still swigging his cigar as he goes. I'm glad I came in my own car. Once again, I might not be good for a lift home.

Nothing but grey clouds and rain

My great Aunty Eily, Grandma Alexander's eldest sister who lives in England, has sent me a postcard with fields of daffodils and a quote from William Shakespeare's sonnet:

Shall I compare thee to a summer's day?

Thou art more lovely and more temperate:

Rough winds do shake the darling buds of May,

And summer's lease hath all too short a date;

How wrong can she be? There certainly aren't any darling buds of May here in Hampstead. Yesterday it snowed. This morning when I look out of the window, the sky is grey and it's raining. On my arrival at the Cumberland Tennis Club in Hampstead, although the courts look like mud baths, the officials insist we go on. It drizzles all the way through the match, but in England they only stop play when the puddles get too deep, one of the other players tells me, otherwise they wouldn't finish the tournaments. By the middle of the third set, I feel and look like a drenched rat. My tennis skirt and top are soaking wet, the balls are sodden masses of yellow fur and my racket handle keeps slipping around in my hand. Worse still, I lose, albeit narrowly in the third set to an English player, Alex Soady. At least the bloody rain stops anyone noticing my tears as I come off the court.

Chapter 66

DE GUATEMALA A GUATEPEOR

It doesn't take Mum and Dad long to notice that things are not all "roses in the garden" between Pedro and me. Pedro's behaviour has gone progressively downhill even when Mum and Dad are at our place. The tension in the air is palpable. Since his cousin Alvaro decamped back to Bonar, Pedro is right back to his old obsessive self in regard to cleanliness, tidiness, personal grooming and, of course, dust. I have to laugh. Even Dad, who's never done a skerrick of housework in his entire life that I've ever seen, madly races around with the hot pink feather duster whenever he hears the lift coming up, announcing Pedro's return from the stock exchange.

Dad, who is renowned in the family for spending long periods in the toilet (it was to do with his English nanny's toilet training), tells me that he can't believe how long Pedro spends in the bathroom.

"And he doesn't even take the newspaper in with him," he adds.

A couple of weeks into Mum and Dad's stay, Pedro explodes, losing it completely, then drives off into the night and doesn't come back for three days. During this period, we don't hear a word from him. He finally appears late on the third day with a large gash over his eye "from a car crash".

"I have to steel myself not to fall over laughing," Dad tells me when Pedro goes into the bathroom to clean up. "He certainly lives up to his Latin temperament. You sure can pick 'em, Sucat. I'm never quite sure what's going to happen next!"

Dad is not the only one.

"I don't know what attracted you to him in the first place," Mum pipes in. "The only thing I can see you both have in common, after careful examination of your relationship over the last couple of months, is that you both eat copious amounts of garlic."

Mum is always going on about how couples should have "things in common". In the past, I'd always thought that her theory sounded boring. But maybe she has a point. Pedro's and my differences are certainly stretching me to the limit, not to mention Mum and Dad, who are almost at breaking point.

Mum and Dad certainly look a bit the worse for wear when they arrive the following morning. They report that they haven't managed to get much sleep during the night.

"The Spaniards are a bloody noisy race," Dad complains. "Especially late at night, or should I say, early in the morning." I try not to giggle. "The comings and goings well after midnight in the apartment block where we are staying are quite unbelievable. Their loud voices, giggling, the noise of the lift, not to mention the number of times the toilet chain is pulled, penetrate the walls of our flat, which are like cardboard. You'd think they could be a bit more considerate."

I'm not surprised. Poor Mum and Dad. It is a well-known fact that the apartments in the Calle Dr Fleming block where they are staying is where the Spanish men keep their mistresses and that's why leases are available on a monthly basis. Their long-suffering wives seem to turn a blind eye to these arrangements, as well as to their husbands' nocturnal activities, as long as they return to their own home by the end of the night and, of course, attend Mass with their wives and family on Sundays, Saints days, at Easter and Christmas.

When Pedro leaves for the stock exchange, Dad corners me in the kitchen. "The other reason why I haven't been able to sleep is that I'm worried about you, Sucat. I can see that things between you and Pedro aren't all that rosy," he tells me. Well that's to put it mildly, I think. "I want to organise a family meeting to discuss what can be done to rectify the situation."

"I reckon I've tried everything," I burst out. "I really can't see what else I can do! I've been sweet, I've tried to jolly him, I've ignored him, I've tried to reason with him and I've even yelled at him, but none of these tactics have done an ounce of good. Pedro is just an impossible person to live with."

And somehow I don't think that he is going to take too kindly to Dad's suggestion of a family meeting. In Spain, husbands are kings and nobody dares question their authority.

Later in the day, when Pedro arrives home, I cringe in the kitchen while Dad tries to explain to him about his idea of a family meeting. Pedro doesn't appear to be getting too many of the finer points because his English is still not much chop. I can hear Dad speaking louder and louder. For some reason he seems to think that Pedro will eventually understand what he says if he increases the volume. Dad sets the family meeting down for the next day at 11am.

"*Las once*," dad says holding up both his hands with his fingers splayed and then afterwards, one finger. Mum and Dad have been taking Spanish lessons at a local college since their arrival but Dad, like Pedro, isn't a natural with languages.

The next day when we all sit around the table things go from bad to disastrous.

"Now Pedro, what is the problem exactly between you and Sue?" Dad starts off by asking, while I feel like I want to slide under the table.

"When I first see Susanna," Pedro answers, "I think she eez an angel but I find zees eez not true. She eez a devil." This stumps even Dad for a few minutes. "She eez not good wife like Thelma," Pedro continues.

I'm not sure if he is referring to my housekeeping skills, or the fact that I don't buckle under and take orders as I should.

Even Dad in the end starts to think that the meeting is not heading anywhere and is in fact a lost cause. At that particular point, Pedro goes off in a huff.

"Things don't look good, Sucat," says Dad, an eternal optimist, who normally *never* admits defeat. "My next step is to seek some legal advice in order to find out what your rights are here in Spain, because once Thelma and I go back home to Australia, it will be much more difficult for us to help you."

Queens Club Championships

My billet, Colonel Hudson, picks me up at Green Park station in a cab. We go for lunch at a very posh restaurant in Piccadilly called Maisies. I am not dressed for the occasion. A supercilious waiter flashes me a look of disdain before briskly stowing my battered luggage out of sight. The menu is complex. I'm at a loss what to choose. I decide to go along with whatever Colonel Hudson orders. I pray he doesn't pick steak tartar. I've already been caught out with that one in Monte Carlo. After lunch, we catch a taxi to his flat in Little St James Street, right on top of Pruniers. He tells me he has two grace and favour apartments for services to the Queen. As the other two girls staying here aren't arriving until tomorrow I place a chair under the door handle. How strange the English are that they billet a young single girl with an elderly bachelor. Mum and Dad would have a fit!

Chapter 67

UNA REUNION CON EL ABOGADO

The next morning, I just manage to grab the phone before Pedro answers it on his way out the door. I wave him off.

"*Es papa!*" I tell him.

"Ask around at the tennis club for the name of a good lawyer," Dad says.

This is going to be a bit of a worry. How am I going to manage it without anyone twigging to what is going on? In the end I decide to ask Senor Boni, the club manager, because he knows everything about everyone. Of course, as I suspected, he naturally wants to know what kind of lawyer Dad is looking for.

"Just for general legal work," I tell him, trying to fob him off by being as vague as possible. Someone who speaks good English," I add, hoping he'll think that maybe Dad is going to buy a property or an investment.

He recommends Fernando Escardo from the firm of Bufete Jose Mario Armero Alcantara.

"They are excellent lawyers," he says. "And Fernando went to uni in England so he speaks very good English."

With a firm name like that I bet they charge like a wounded bull, I surmise. The following morning, I have to wait for Pedro to go to the stock exchange before I can ring and make an appointment with the lawyers. When he finally leaves I am shaking like a leaf. I pick up the phone and only just manage to squeeze my voice out of my throat.

The offices of Bufete Jose Mario Armero Alcantara are situated in a grand old building, commensurate with their name, on the 6th floor, in the Calle de Recoletos 22 just off Calle de Serano. After only a short wait in the reception area, we are shown into a huge, old room with high ceilings. The walls are lined from floor to ceiling with shelves crammed to the hilt with well-worn leather-bound books. The lawyer who greets us, a dapper little man, not much over five feet, is dwarfed by his huge old desk, which is covered with files and papers. And of course, us!

"Permit me to introduce myself. I am Juan del Carre. I will be preparing the brief of the case on behalf of Senor Escardo," he states.

He then starts telling us how he rides to work on a push-bike which he attaches to a telephone pole with a chain just outside his office while he is at work. I am sure he's going on with this preamble to ease the tension, which feels like it has almost exhausted the available oxygen supply in the room. He insists that we go over to the window to check it out, and sure enough, there is a push-bike attached by a chain directly below.

After we've dutifully admired his bike, he begins by asking, "So, tell me exactly what the problem is."

I am very embarrassed and feel like a naughty child being discussed by her parents as Dad goes over the situation between Pedro and me.

"From what I can see, it is largely a matter of cultural differences, which are creating the major part of the problem," Dad says. "Pedro, Sue's husband, probably just has the normal expectations of a Spanish husband. However, things are very different in Australia for married women. They can come and go as they like, and husbands, in general, are not so particular about the standard of housework. Sue has been on a freer rein than most girls, even Australian ones, travelling around Europe, playing tennis over the last couple of years. The adjustment to the life of a Spanish housewife for her, in my opinion, is improbable. The volatility of the Spanish temperament is also very different from the laid-back Australian one."

"I am not at all surprised by what you're telling me," Juan del Carre says. "When I was young and single, I too fell in love with a very beautiful Australian girl, who was a ballerina. I desperately wanted to marry her, but in the end, due to pressure from my parents, I didn't, and although I was absolutely heartbroken at the time, in the long run, I think it was probably for the best."

Dad is well prepared for the meeting and has compiled a list of questions. It is lucky that one of the team is on the ball because I am experiencing a complete mental blackout and a feeling of total unreality about the whole proceedings. Dad gets right down to the nitty-gritty by asking whether I would be able to take Alex out of the country legally and could the marriage between Pedro and me be dissolved in any way.

Juan responds that initially he would need to do some research and also confer with Fernando prior to giving us any advice or recommendations about what actions to take.

"And so that we can conduct the necessary investigations into the matter, would you please give me the date of birth of the child, Alexander, and the address of the hospital or sanatorium where the delivery took place, and the names of the parties involved. I will also require the date and address where the marriage ceremony took place?" he requests, as he relieves Dad of his list of questions.

When we meet again with our lawyer a week later, he tells us on our arrival at his office that he has discovered something about Pedro which would never have dawned on me in my wildest dreams.

"The judge who performed the marriage ceremony at the address you gave me is from the Provincia de Leon. He does not have the jurisdiction to act in this capacity in Madrid."

"What does that mean exactly?" Dad interrupts.

"I'll get to that in a minute," replies Juan del Carre. "The most important piece of information that I want to relay to you is that Pedro was already married prior to this ceremony taking place."

We are all stunned.

"We have obtained an authenticated photocopy by a public notary of the relevant pages of the passport of Pedro Rivera de Flores, whose personal description includes mention of the fact that his civil status is *married*. The said passport is dated 4 February 1970, which is just over two years ago. Obviously, this is prior to your daughter and Pedro meeting. It is really difficult," he continues, "for us to obtain the marriage certificate of Pedro Rivera de Flores, because there is no central civil registry in Spain, only thousands of municipal registries. This kind of search is extremely difficult to make, unless we are given the place and date when Senor Rivera de Flores contracted the marriage, as well as the maiden name of his wife."

I am totally shocked, unable to utter a word. I have to admit that I have seen Pedro's passport before, when I grabbed it from him once to try to find out how old he was. But when I questioned him about his civil status of "married", he told me that he'd been travelling around with an English air hostess at the time, and it made it easier to book into hotels. And because I had heard so many stories of the bribery and corruption that goes on under the current regime, like people getting their marriage annulled for non-consummation, even though they had four children, I believed him.

Our solicitor goes on to advise that under Spanish law I don't have any custodial rights over Alex even though Pedro and I aren't legally married and he in fact is a bigamist. Spain is a patriarchal society. As a woman, I don't have any rights at all, it seems.

"My advice to you is that you need to make arrangements to leave Spain with the baby as soon as you can. I really can't see any alternative. The only piece of good news," he continues, "is that Pedro hasn't registered Alex's birth, which I believe will make it easier for you to get him onto your Australian passport and out of the country."

"A standing prick hath no conscience," Dad mutters under his breath as we make our way along the street.

It is one of Mum's favourite sayings, from the Latin proverb *penis erectus non habet conscientiam*. In other words, if a man has a hard-on he won't stop at anything to get what he wants.

The Wengen International

The Swiss sky is cobalt blue, the air crisp and it is whisper quiet. There are no cars here in Wengen. I'm staying in the most beautiful room at the Palace Hotel with its own bathroom! Each morning I wake to the ringing of cowbells. A maid delivers my breakfast of wonderful hot breads and pastries in a cane basket, with a jug of freshly squeezed orange juice and a pot of milk coffee. I eat on the balcony overlooking the valley with snow-capped mountains in the distance. It is an exciting week. I dance every night with a handsome Mauritian, Rolande de Trevou, to Strauss walzes. Despite all these late nights and the difficulty of playing in high altitude, I win the tournament. On the last morning, there's a kerfuffle in the street below. The boys, who've been drinking up a storm all week, try to nick out without paying their drinks bill. They're being herded back to the hotel at rifle point by a caretaker!

Chapter 68

NOS ESCAPAMOS

I receive a warm welcome when I go to the Australian Embassy. All the people I've met before come out of their offices to say hello and admire Alex. Although he is still tiny, he now has beautiful olive skin, large soulful dark brown eyes and a small thatch of blonde hair. In a way I suppose I am lucky that I've already met many of the staff who work here beforehand—I've no doubt this helps to smooth the way. They don't suspect anything when I tell them that I've lost my passport. I just have to sign a stat dec to that effect. The truth is that it is still locked in Pedro's safe, together with the huge diamond ring he gave me for a wedding present.

Most fortunately for me, it turns out that under Australian law, children under two travel on their mother's passport. From that moment on, little Alex is no longer Alejandro Jon Rivera de Flores. He is now Alexander Jon Alexander.

A couple of days later, Dad tells me that everything is all set for our departure. He's picked up Alex's and my tickets for London. Up until now, everything that has been happening seems unreal, but the fact that Dad has now purchased our tickets does bring things back to earth. Initially, Pedro doesn't seem to notice that anything is going on. I suppose he is relaxed because I have Mum and Dad in tow with me all the time. I also have intermittent wet patches on the front of my blouse, which no doubt in his mind, would surely deter even the most ardent prospective lover I may be considering entering into a dalliance with.

However, as the week wears on he starts to twig that something is afoot. He notices that I am jumpy and nervous at the slightest thing and keep breaking out in hot sweats. My heart starts racing whenever I contemplate what is going to happen. And as usual when I am under nervous strain I have a bad attack of the runs. The week is the longest in my life, seeming to stretch to eternity. I don't know how I live through the last few days and fervently wish I could take a leap into the future, just by-passing them completely.

While Pedro is at the stock exchange the day before we leave, I pack all my clothes and things that I will need. I have to make some tough decisions on what I can and can't take. There is no way I can possibly remove all my clothes without Pedro noticing. Some things I dearly love will have to stay hanging in the wardrobe in Madrid. It is a terrible shame, but I also have to leave behind Mum's original copy of the *Commonsense Cookery Book* which had taken pride of place in the kitchen all during my childhood, and has proved such a boon to my limited cooking skills since she presented me with it. I also have to forgo all the beautiful Corningware casserole dishes and elegant crystal glassware that I'd won in hard fought battles in my teen years at country tournaments which Mum had carefully packed and brought over with her to Madrid. So that the wardrobe doesn't look too empty, I re-hang the flowing maternity dresses which I'd purchased when

I first found out I was pregnant, but because Alex came so early, have never worn.

It is all set for us to leave the next day. Mum and Dad have arranged to take Alex for the night so Pedro and I can go to the movies. In reality it is so I'll have one less thing to worry about in the morning when I make my escape. Pedro keeps me up to the early hours of the morning with question after question. He tells me he knows that something is going on and keeps on asking me what is happening. As luck would have it, he is nowhere near the mark, but sometimes near enough, that I am very close to blabbing. I only just manage to keep the brakes on. I am almost delirious by the finish. But in the back of my mind lurks the fact that Dad would kill me if I spilt the beans now. This little exercise has cost him a fortune, not to mention the stress he and Mum have undergone. Somehow in the end, I manage to placate Pedro and remind him that I have to play in an important tennis match the following day and need my sleep.

In the morning I have cold shivers running up and down my body, trembling hands and heartbeats so strong I feel they are going to burst right through my chest, as well as a continuation of the "runs". When I go down to the garage to drive my ever-faithful Fiat 500 round to pick up Mum, Dad and Alex, it won't start. Although sometimes in cold weather it can be sluggish, this is the first time it has let me down completely. It has always been the most wonderful little car. The poor darling must know that it is about to be abandoned, its fate cast to wind.

Jose Maria, the *portero*, who is down in the garage, comes and gives me a hand by pushing the car. Somehow I manage to clutch-start it going down the drive, even though I am shaking all over. He will be lucky to keep his job when Pedro finds out about this little effort, but I don't dare warn him.

As arranged, Mum and Dad are waiting in the vestibule of their apartment with Alex, all ready to go. I dart in quickly to help them with their luggage, leaving the car running. I don't want to risk it not starting again. We only just manage to squeeze all their suitcases and bags into the boot, the overflow in the back seat and below Dad's feet in the front. Our noses are practically on the windscreen. In the end, we have to leave Alex's pram behind. There's just no way we can get it in. The drive to the airport is a nightmare. My arms tingle, my heart is racing, my knees have all but disappeared which makes it very difficult to change gears. I keep checking the rear-vision mirror to see if there are any green Mustangs in hot pursuit. I am so nervous my throat constricts, making it almost impossible to speak. Mum and Dad must feel the same because we don't exchange a single word the whole way. I'm really concerned that Dad's blood pressure won't be able to withstand the strain. Mum and I are both worried he'll have another stroke. As there is not as much traffic as usual, we arrive at Barajas Airport with heaps of time to spare. Plenty of time for more nerves to kick in.

I feel very sad when I farewell my little car for the last time, leaving it unlocked with the keys in the ignition. I guess the dreaded *grua* (council tow truck) will come and take it away. Once inside the airport, when we go to give Alex his feed, we discover that Mum, in her haste, has left Alex's precious formula on the table in their apartment. Luckily we manage to buy some tinned milk. It's the best we can do.

We are all in total panic mode as we wait what seems like forever for our British Airline flight to London to be called. To make matters worse, it is announced that our flight will be delayed an hour and a half due to bad weather during the flight from London. We sit in the waiting area, every moment expecting the worst. Every time someone walks towards us, my heart thumps. Mum and Dad both look decidedly green around the gills. Their eyes are continually scanning the airport—expecting Pedro's entrance at any minute. Fortunately, after his bottle of the tinned milk, Alex sleeps the whole time.

At last they call us to board. We only just sit down and buckle in, when there is a further announcement that there is some other kind of hold-up and our flight is to be delayed again. I pray fervently that it isn't anything to do with us. Fortunately, Mum and Dad are totally unaware of the reputation the Guardia de Civil has for plonking people, especially foreigners, in jail and keeping them there indefinitely without them being allowed to notify anyone or have legal representation. *They* are just worried about being confronted by an angry Pedro. We all sit there, sweating it out once again, until at long last an elegantly-suited fat gentleman runs across the tarmac, briefcase in hand, races up the gangway and plops down in the first-class section. We hold our collective breaths. Finally, the stairs are drawn up and the engines fired, we speed across the tarmac and are airborne. All three of us breathe huge sighs of relief.

To be continued…